The MAILBOX®

Hooray for Dramatic Play!

30 Fun-Filled Themes for Your Play Area

 Inspire creative and imaginative play

 Encourage cooperation and sharing

 Promote language development

 Invite active problem solving

Managing Editor: Brenda Fay

Editorial Team: Becky S. Andrews, Diane Badden, Kimberley Bruck, Karen A. Brudnak, Pam Crane, Sarah Foreman, Tazmen Hansen, Marsha Heim, Lori Z. Henry, Lucia Kemp Henry, Sheila Krill, Debra Liverman, Kitty Lowrance, Kimberly Murphy, Tina Petersen, Mark Rainey, Kelly Robertson, Hope Rodgers, Rebecca Saunders, Leanne S. Swinson, Rachael Traylor, Sharon M. Tresino, Zane Williard

www.themailbox.com

©2011 The Mailbox® Books
All rights reserved.
ISBN10 #1-56234-978-3 • ISBN13 #978-1-56234-978-3

Printed in the United States
10 9 8 7 6 5 4 3 2 1

HPS 227018

Table of Contents

What's Inside

For each play theme, get...

an easy-to-follow plan,

Camping Site

1. Choose props

Camping Supplies

- checklist (page 28)
- small dome tent
- sleeping bag or blanket and pillow
- outdoor camping apparel
- play campfire (see tip)
- empty food boxes and containers
- play food
- pots and frying pan
- cooking utensils
- plastic plates and cutlery
- baking rack atop a lidless box with tissue paper flames (grill)
- napkins
- cooler
- flashlight or lantern
- toy first aid kit with adhesive bandages and gauze

Fishing Supplies

- craft foam fish with magnetic tape attached
- large pond-shaped cutout
- small outdoor chair
- magnetic fishing pole
- tackle box
- plastic pail

Hiking Supplies

- sign (page 27)
- bird cutouts or pictures (displayed around the room)
- toy forest animals
- map
- compass
- toy binoculars
- toy camera
- backpacks
- empty water bottles

Tip!
To make a campfire, glue cardboard tubes (logs) to a cardboard base; then glue tissue paper flames to the logs. Surround the fire with medium-size rocks or wads of gray paper.

2. Introduce the theme

Maisy Goes Camping by Lucy Cousins

Camping Fun
Let's go and pitch our tent
At the perfect campsite.
We'll make a cozy fire
That has flames so tall and bright.
We'll sing songs and tell stories,
And we'll roast marshmallows too.
Then it will be time to sleep.
Camping's fun for me and you!

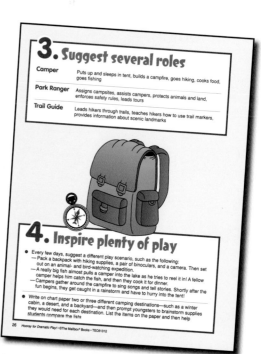

3. Suggest several roles

Camper	Puts up and sleeps in tent, builds a campfire, goes hiking, cooks food, goes fishing
Park Ranger	Assigns campsites, assists campers, protects animals and land, enforces safety rules, leads tours
Trail Guide	Leads hikers through trails, teaches hikers how to use trail markers, provides information about scenic landmarks

4. Inspire plenty of play

- Every few days, suggest a different play scenario, such as the following:
  — Pack a backpack with hiking supplies, a pair of binoculars, and a camera. Then set out on an animal- and bird-watching expedition.
  — A really big fish almost pulls a camper into the lake as he tries to reel it in! A fellow camper helps him catch the fish, and then they cook it for dinner.
  — Campers gather around the campfire to sing songs and tell stories. Shortly after the fun begins, they get caught in a rainstorm and have to hurry into the tent!
- Write on chart paper two or three different camping destinations—such as a winter cabin, a desert, and a backyard—and then prompt youngsters to brainstorm supplies they would need for each destination. List the items on the paper and then help students compare the lists.

a mini poster, and a bonus prop!

Hiking Trail

Camping Checklist

- ☐ sleeping bag
- ☐ camera
- ☐ tent
- ☐ binoculars
- ☐ food
- ☐ map
- ☐ flashlight
- ☐ compass
- ☐ fishing pole
- ☐ first aid kit

Hooray for Dramatic Play! • ©The Mailbox® Books • TEC61312

Airport

1. Choose props

Passenger Supplies

luggage
books/magazines
toy camera
dolls (children)

Check-In Supplies

airline sign (page 7)
tickets (page 8)
travel posters and brochures
luggage tags
telephone

Airplane Supplies

chairs (arranged in rows)
dark-color blazer (for flight attendant uniform)
serving trays
clean, empty soda bottles
paper cups
napkins
empty individual-serving snack packages
play food
small pillows
small blankets
magazines

Tip!
Contact a local travel agency and ask them to donate unneeded travel posters and brochures.

2. Introduce the theme

 Airport by Byron Barton

Off We Go!
(sung to the tune of "Yankee Doodle")

It's time to climb aboard the plane.
It's so much fun to fly.
When we are all buckled in,
We'll zoom into the sky.

We will fly up through the air.
Through the clouds, we'll glide.
Oh what fun we will have.
I love this airplane ride.

3. Suggest several roles

Counter Attendant	Sells tickets, checks in passengers, tags luggage, answers questions, calls passengers to board plane
Passenger	Buys ticket, checks in, asks questions, boards plane, follows flight attendant's instructions, eats snacks or meals, reads magazines or books
Baggage Handler	Puts luggage on plane prior to flight, takes luggage off plane after it lands
Flight Attendant	Helps passengers find their seats, gives safety instructions prior to takeoff, serves food and beverages, assists passengers with other needs
Pilot	Flies plane, announces information over loudspeaker

4. Inspire plenty of play

● Every few days, suggest a different play scenario, such as the following:
  — Holiday time is here. The airport is filled with people traveling to visit family.
  — Passengers are seat belted and ready for takeoff, but the plane won't start. Airport workers assist passengers in switching to a different plane.
  — Passengers are on a long flight to Australia and the babies are getting cranky. The flight attendants sing songs to help quiet the restless passengers.

● Encourage youngsters to make travel posters featuring places they would like to visit; then invite students to share their posters during group time. If desired, display the posters in the center.

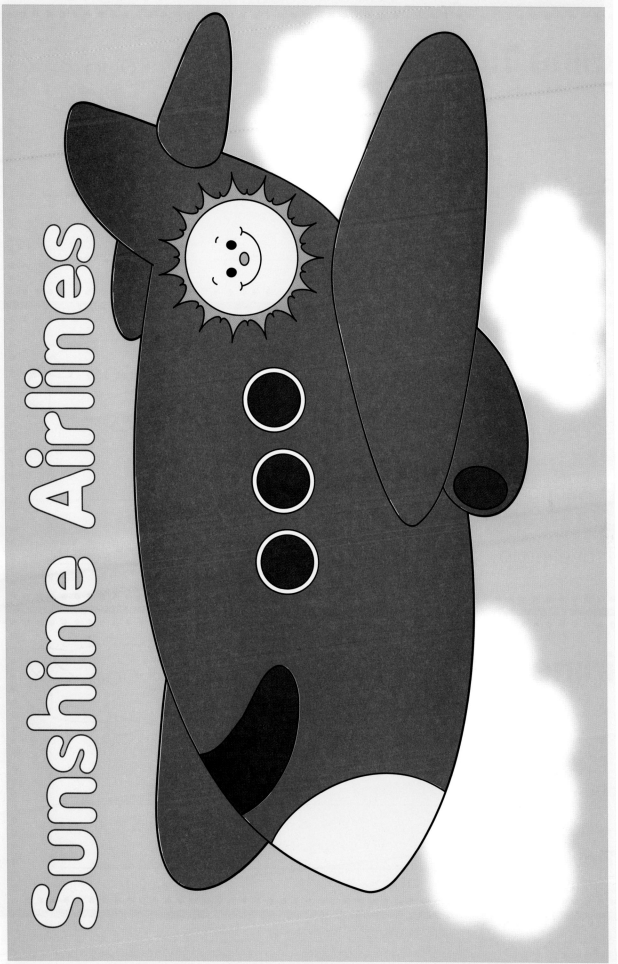

Sunshine Airlines

Hooray for Dramatic Play! • ©The Mailbox® Books • TEC61312

Note to the teacher: Use with pages 5 and 6. Make a copy of page 8 for your files. Remove this mini poster and put it in a plastic page protector for durability. Then display it at the center at students' eye level.

Airline Ticket

Passenger _____

Traveling to _____

Airline Ticket

Passenger _____

Traveling to _____

Airline Ticket

Passenger _____

Traveling to _____

Hooray for Dramatic Play! • ©The Mailbox® Books • TEC61312

Note to the teacher: Use with pages 5 and 6. To save paper, laminate one or two copies of this page and cut the tickets apart. Provide the same number of wipe-off markers as the number of tickets.

Bakery

1. Choose props

Kitchen Supplies

apron
baker's hat
mixing bowl
large mixing spoon
measuring cups and spoons
rolling pin
cookie cutters
baking trays and pans
cupcake liners
oven mitts
spatula
plastic knives
tongs
serving tray

Baking Ingredients

clean, empty ingredient containers, such as
those for flour, sugar, baking powder, oil,
and milk
sterilized egg cartons with plastic eggs

empty plastic spice jars
plastic or craft foam fruit (for pies)
play dough

Decorating Supplies

clean, empty icing containers
craft foam flower shapes
empty candy sprinkles containers

Business Supplies

bakery sign (page 11)
order forms (page 12)
money-related props (pages 125–128)
toy cash register
telephone
boxes and bags (for packing baked goods)
latex-free food service gloves

Tip!
Ask the owner of a local bakery
if she would donate a few unused
bakery boxes.

2. Introduce the theme

 Mr. Cookie Baker by Monica Wellington

 Tempting Treats
*(sung to the tune of the chorus
of "Jingle Bells")*

Cakes and pies,
Doughnuts, bread,
Cookies big and small.
Come out to our bakery.
You'll want to buy them all!
(Repeat.)

3. Suggest several roles

Baker	Mixes ingredients and bakes cookies, pies, cakes, doughnuts, and bread
Bakery Clerk	Answers telephone, takes orders, serves customers, collects customers' payments, refills trays with baked goods, cleans counters
Customer	Places orders, purchases baked goods

4. Inspire plenty of play

- Every few days, suggest a different play scenario, such as the following:
  - The bakery is flooded with orders for birthday celebrations! The bakers are working hard to fill birthday cake and cupcake orders.
  - Cookies are on a special sale today and tomorrow. Buy one cookie and get one free!
  - There is a parade starting at 9 AM. The bakers are busy making doughnuts to prepare for the breakfast rush.
  - Pies are the popular pastry this week. The bakers are trying different ingredients to create new and unique pies.

- Set out a few bakery foods—such as doughnuts, pastries, and cookies—and then invite students to taste the items. After the taste test is finished, have youngsters complete a graph to see if there is a class favorite.

Busy Bakery

Hooray for Dramatic Play! • ©The Mailbox® Books • TEC61312

Note to the teacher: Use with pages 9 and 10. Make a copy of page 12 for your files. Remove this mini poster and put it in a plastic page protector for durability. Then display it at the center at students' eye level.

Special Order

Bakery Item	How Many?
☐ cookies 	_____
☐ cake 	_____
☐ muffins 	_____
☐ pie 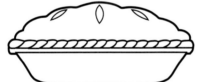	_____
☐ doughnuts 	_____

Customer's name _____

Hooray for Dramatic Play! • ©The Mailbox® Books • TEC61312

Note to the teacher: Use with pages 9 and 10. To save paper, laminate one or two copies of this page and provide an equal number of wipe-off markers. To place an order, a child checks the box next to each desired baked good and then writes each quantity on the line.

Beach

1. Choose props

Beach Supplies

beach sign (page 15)
blue bedsheet (ocean)
clear, shallow tub filled with sand
seashells
toy sea creatures
chair (for lifeguard)

Beachgoer Supplies

checklist (page 16)
music player and a recording of lively music
small beach chair
beach bag
sun hat or visor
sunglasses
beach towel
clean, empty sunscreen bottle
flip-flops

sand toys, such as a plastic pail and shovel
float ring
beach ball
beach-themed books
cooler stocked with play food
toy camera
clean, empty water bottles
spray bottle filled with water

Tip!
Ask parents and coworkers for donations of medium and large seashells.

2. Introduce the theme

 Beach Day written by Karen Roosa and illustrated by Maggie Smith

We Are Going to the Beach
(sung to the tune of "If You're Happy and You Know It")

Oh, we're going to the beach. Hip, hip, hooray! Hooray!
We'll have fun out in the sun. Hip, hip, hooray! Hooray!
We will run along the shore
And find pretty shells galore!
We are going to the beach. Hip, hip, hooray! Hooray!

3. Suggest several roles

Lifeguard	Observes swimmers, provides help when needed
Beach Patrol Officer	Observes beachgoers to make sure they are safe, enforces beach rules
Beachgoer	Swims in ocean, plays on beach, builds sand castles, collects seashells, reads, eats

4. Inspire plenty of play

- Every few days, suggest a different play scenario, such as the following:
  - Lots of seashells washed up on the beach overnight. Beachgoers go on a seashell hunt. Then each person counts his shells to see who collected the most.
  - A sign has been posted for a sand castle–building contest today. Beachgoers must sign an entry sheet to participate. Then they build their best sand castles.
  - Beachgoers set out a perfect picnic. While they are eating, a huge wave comes ashore and washes all the food into the ocean.
  - Join other beachgoers for a dance party at the beach!

- Conceal beach-related items in a tote bag. A child removes an item from the bag, names it, and then explains how it is related to the beach.

Ready for the Sun

Sunscreen

Hooray for Dramatic Play! • ©The Mailbox® Books • TEC61312

Note to the teacher: Use with pages 13 and 14. Make a copy of page 16 for your files. Remove this mini poster and put it in a plastic sheet protector for durability. Then display it at the center at students' eye level. Have youngsters refer to the poster to make sure they have the necessary items to protect themselves from the sun.

Beach Trip Checklist

☐ sunglasses

☐ towel

☐ sun visor

☐ float ring

☐ sunscreen

☐ camera

☐ sand toys

☐ water

☐ flip-flops

☐ cooler

Hooray for Dramatic Play! • ©The Mailbox® Books • TEC61312

Note to the teacher: Use with pages 13 and 14. To save paper, laminate one or two copies of this page and provide an equal number of wipe-off markers.

Birthday Party

1. Choose props

Preparation Supplies

invitations (page 20)
paper plates, bowls, and cups
plastic utensils
napkins
crepe paper streamers
birthday banner
Mylar balloons (attached to the wall)

Gift Supplies

gift bags
tissue paper
boxes
wrapping paper
tape
gift bows
toys (presents)
birthday cards

Party Supplies

"Where's the Nose?" (page 19)
white foam rectangle or square (see tip)
birthday candles
party hats
play food
clean, empty soda or juice bottles
clean, empty ice cream container
ice cream scooper
music player and a recording of music
noisemakers
goody bags (with toy)
toy camera

Tip!
To make a cake, press candles into a foam rectangle and then glue on decorations.

2. Introduce the theme

 Birthday Zoo written by Deborah Lee Rose and illustrated by Lynn Munsinger

 Birthday Party Plans
(sung to the tune of "Frère Jacques")

It's my birthday.
It's my birthday.
Won't you come
Have some fun?
Have an ice cream treat
And some cake to eat.
I can't wait!
Don't be late.

3. Suggest several roles

Birthday Child   Greets guests, plays games, eats birthday treats, opens presents, hands out goody bags, thanks guests for coming

Guest   Brings present, eats birthday treats, plays games, thanks birthday child for inviting her

Parent   Sets up party decorations, buys or makes birthday treats, drops off or greets guests, supervises party, serves birthday treats

4. Inspire plenty of play

- Every few days, suggest a different play scenario, such as the following:
  — Youngsters secretly plan a surprise birthday party for someone special.
  — Partygoers chip in and buy one really big gift. They have to wrap the huge gift and figure out how to get it to the birthday party.
  — Compose a fun song to sing to the birthday person before eating the tasty birthday treats.
  — Today's birthday celebration includes rhythm instruments and a parade.

- During group time, explain that having a birthday means you are growing and getting older. Display pictures of living and nonliving things. Then invite youngsters to tell which things will grow and get older, which ones will not, and why.

Where's the Nose?

Hooray for Dramatic Play! • ©The Mailbox® Books • TEC61312

Note to the teacher: Use with pages 17 and 18. Make a copy of page 20 for your files. Remove this mini poster and laminate it for durability. Then display it in a student-accessible location. Nearby, place several paper circles (noses) and Sticky-Tac adhesive. To use the poster, each child attaches a small piece of adhesive to the back of a nose. Then, with adult supervision, youngsters play Stick the Nose on the Clown (similar to Pin the Tail on the Donkey).

19

You're Invited to a Party!

For: _____

Date: _____

Time: _____

TEC61312

You're Invited to a Party!

For: _____

Date: _____

Time: _____

TEC61312

Hooray for Dramatic Play! • ©The Mailbox® Books • TEC61312

Note to the teacher: Use with pages 17 and 18. To save paper, laminate a few copies of this page and provide an equal number of wipe-off markers.

Business Office

1. Choose props

General Office Supplies

office sign (page 23)
tables or desks
chairs
empty office-supply boxes
calendar

Supplies for Each Desk

envelopes
stickers (stamps)
old computer keyboard
magazine page in an 8" x 10" acrylic frame
  (computer monitor—see tip)
pencil cup containing pens, pencils, and
  highlighters
paper
paper tray
notepads
sticky notes
tape dispenser
stapler (with adult supervision)
calculator

Secretary Supplies

supply order form (page 24)
money-related props (pages 125–128)
telephone
telephone book
appointment book
file folders
junk mail

Waiting Area Supplies

chairs
magazines
toy coffee pot
plastic pitcher (for water)
disposable cups

Tip!
Periodically change the magazine page in the acrylic frame to add variety.

2. Introduce the theme

 Daddy Goes to Work, written by Jabari Asim and illustrated by Aaron Boyd

 Business Letters
(sung to the tune of "I've Been Working on the Railroad")

I've been typing business letters
All throughout the day.
I've been typing business letters.
I have to send them on their way.
Don't you hear the keyboard tapping
From morning to afternoon?
I must hurry now and finish.
The day is ending soon!

3. Suggest several roles

Secretary Greets clients and directs them to waiting area, answers telephone, books appointments, files papers, orders supplies, collects payments for services, writes receipts, sorts mail, distributes supplies

Client Reads magazines, drinks coffee or water while waiting, explains needs, fills out forms, asks questions, pays for services

Office Worker Helps clients fill out forms, asks and answers questions, keeps client records, works on computer

4. Inspire plenty of play

- Every few days, suggest a different play scenario, such as the following:
  — The office has been closed several days because of the holidays. Office workers are very busy returning calls and emails.
  — The power went out last night. Office workers are busy checking the computer files to make sure all the information is still there.
  — Office workers hold a meeting to discuss plans for a company picnic.

- Invite parents who work in business offices to visit the class and tell the group about their jobs.

Office Hours
Monday–Friday
9:00–5:00

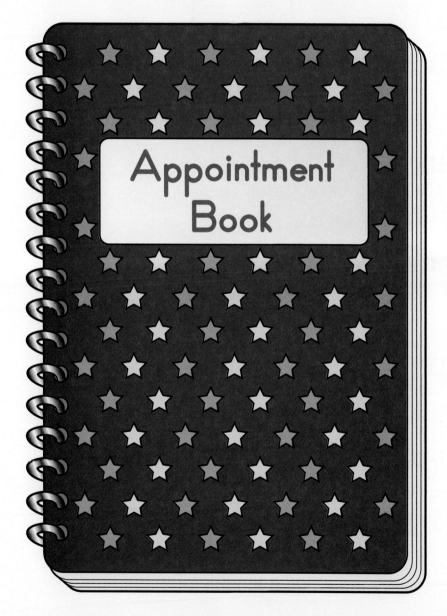

Appointment Book

Call 555-0167 to make an appointment today!

Note to the teacher: Use with pages 21 and 22. Make a copy of page 24 for your files. Remove this mini poster and put it in a plastic page protector for durability. Then display it at the center at students' eye level.

Office Supply Order Form

Item		Amount
☐ paper		_____
☐ envelopes		_____
☐ pencils		_____
☐ pens		_____
☐ tape		_____
☐ folders		_____

Business Name _____

Note to the teacher: Use with pages 21 and 22. To save paper, laminate one or two copies of this page and supply the same number of wipe-off markers.

Camping Site

1. Choose props

Camping Supplies

checklist (page 28)
small dome tent
sleeping bag or blanket and pillow
outdoor camping apparel
play campfire (see tip)
empty food boxes and containers
play food
pots and frying pan
cooking utensils
plastic plates and cutlery
baking rack atop a lidless box with
    tissue paper flames (grill)
napkins
cooler
flashlight or lantern
toy first aid kit with adhesive
    bandages and gauze

Fishing Supplies

craft foam fish with magnetic tape attached
large pond-shaped cutout
small outdoor chair
magnetic fishing pole
tackle box
plastic pail

Hiking Supplies

sign (page 27)
bird cutouts or pictures (displayed around the room)
toy forest animals
map
compass
toy binoculars
toy camera
backpacks
empty water bottles

Tip!
To make a campfire, glue cardboard tubes (logs) to a cardboard base; then glue tissue paper flames to the logs. Surround the fire with medium-size rocks or wads of gray paper.

2. Introduce the theme

 Maisy Goes Camping by Lucy Cousins

Camping Fun
Let's go and pitch our tent
At the perfect campsite.
We'll make a cozy fire
That has flames so tall and bright.
We'll sing songs and tell stories,
And we'll roast marshmallows too.
Then it will be time to sleep.
Camping's fun for me and you!

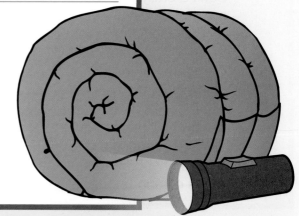

3. Suggest several roles

Camper
Puts up and sleeps in tent, builds a campfire, goes hiking, cooks food, goes fishing

Park Ranger
Assigns campsites, assists campers, protects animals and land, enforces safety rules, leads tours

Trail Guide
Leads hikers through trails, teaches hikers how to use trail markers, provides information about scenic landmarks

4. Inspire plenty of play

- Every few days, suggest a different play scenario, such as the following:
  - Pack a backpack with hiking supplies, a pair of binoculars, and a camera. Then set out on an animal- and bird-watching expedition.
  - A really big fish almost pulls a camper into the lake as he tries to reel it in! A fellow camper helps him catch the fish, and then they cook it for dinner.
  - Campers gather around the campfire to sing songs and tell stories. Shortly after the fun begins, they get caught in a rainstorm and have to hurry into the tent!

- Write on chart paper two or three different camping destinations—such as a winter cabin, a desert, and a backyard—and then prompt youngsters to brainstorm supplies they would need for each destination. List the items on the paper and then help students compare the lists.

Hiking Trail

Note to the teacher: Use with pages 25 and 26. Make a copy of page 28 for your files. Remove this mini poster and put it in a plastic page protector for durability. Then display it at the center at students' eye level.

Camping Checklist

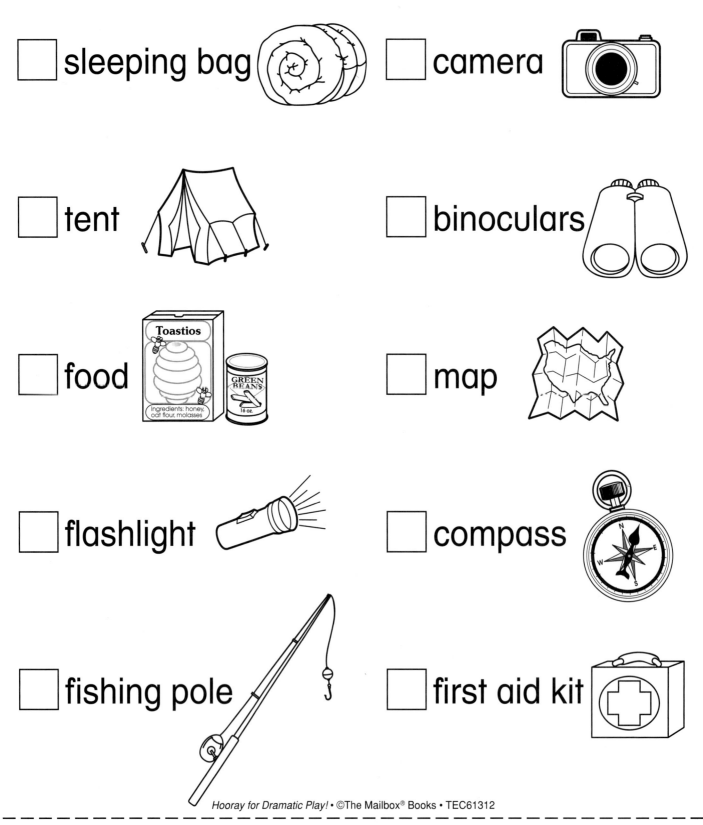

☐ sleeping bag

☐ camera

☐ tent

☐ binoculars

☐ food

Toastios

Ingredients: honey, oat flour, molasses

GREEN BEANS 16 oz.

☐ map

☐ flashlight

☐ compass

☐ fishing pole

☐ first aid kit

Hooray for Dramatic Play! • ©The Mailbox® Books • TEC61312

Note to the teacher: Use with pages 25 and 26. To save paper, laminate one or two copies of this page and supply the same number of wipe-off markers.

Car Repair Shop

1. Choose props

Garage Area Supplies

motor oil bottle labels (page 32)
clean, empty plastic bottles (motor oil bottles)
gas pump (see tip)
chair for car (or make a car from a cardboard box)
repair shop attire, such as work shirts, gloves, and boots
toy toolbox with plastic tools
plastic nuts and bolts
unused gas can
tire gauge
hand-operated air pump
plastic connecting blocks (for making auto parts)
funnel
rags
used car manual

Business Supplies

repair shop sign (page 31)
oil change coupons (page 32)
money-related props (pages 125–128)
toy cash register
telephone
appointment book

Counter and Waiting Area Supplies

chairs
car magazines
auto supply catalog
key rings with keys

Tip!
To make a gas pump, attach a jump rope (hose) to a large cardboard box; then add details to the box.

2. Introduce the theme

♫ **Tune-Up Time**
(sung to the tune of "Shoo Fly")

Clank, clank, something's not tight!
Chug, chug, something's not right.
Off to the fix-it shop.
Oh, please make all this car noise stop!

3. Suggest several roles

Counter Attendant   Answers telephone, greets customers, takes and returns customers' car keys, books appointments, collects payments for services, provides receipts

Customer   Checks in with counter attendant, explains car repair or maintenance service needed, waits while car is being serviced, pays for services

Mechanic   Inspects cars, diagnoses and repairs problems, provides routine maintenance, answers customers' questions, explains work that was done

Zippy Oil

Makes cars happy!

4. Inspire plenty of play

- Every few days, suggest a different play scenario, such as the following:
  — A car breaks down, and the driver calls for roadside assistance. A mechanic from the repair shop comes with tools and fixes the car.
  — Come in for an oil change today or tomorrow and receive a coupon good toward $5.00 off a future oil change.
  — A car is making a funny sound. Several mechanics work together to diagnose and fix the problem.
  — A box of nails fell off a construction truck and spilled all over the road. Vehicles ran over the nails and now several flat tires need to be repaired.
  — Several yearly safety inspections are scheduled for this week.

- Invite youngsters to tell about a time a family car began making a funny noise and needed to go to the repair shop.

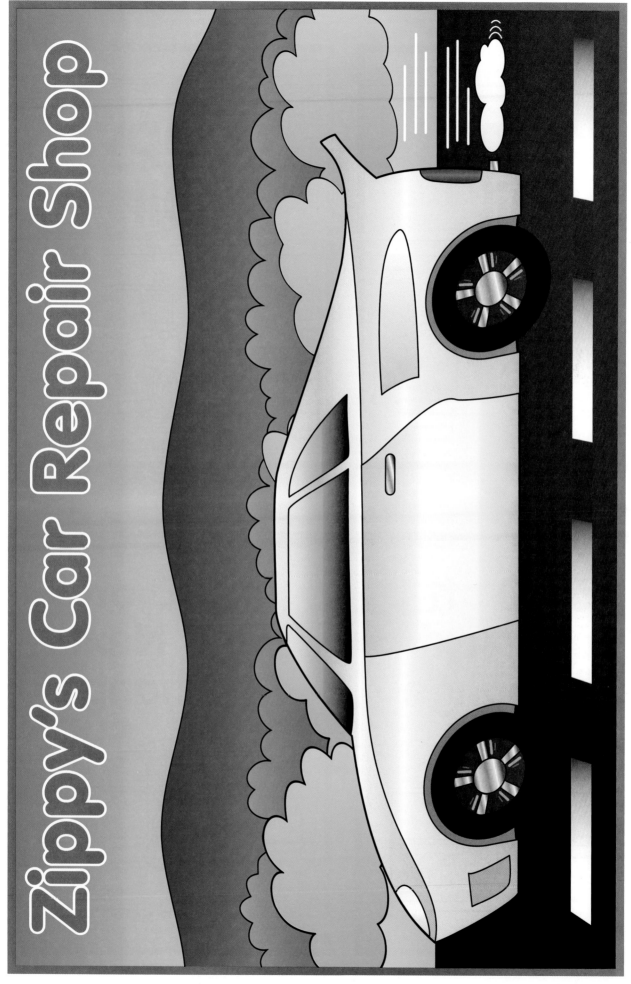

Zippy's Car Repair Shop

Hooray for Dramatic Play! • ©The Mailbox® Books • TEC61312

Note to the teacher: Use with pages 29 and 30. Make a copy of page 32 for your files. Remove this mini poster and put it in a plastic page protector for durability. Then display it at the center at students' eye level.

Motor Oil Bottle Labels
Use with pages 29 and 30.

Zippy Oil

Makes cars happy!

TEC61312

Zippy Oil

Makes cars happy!

TEC61312

Oil Change Coupons
Use with pages 29 and 30.

$5.00 off Your Next Oil Change

Zippy Oil

Makes cars happy!

TEC61312

$5.00 off Your Next Oil Change

Zippy Oil

Makes cars happy!

TEC61312

Car Wash

1. Choose props

Cashier Station Supplies

car wash sign (page 35)
money-related props (pages 125–128)
toy cash register
notepad and pencil (for writing customer
   requests)
key ring with keys
chairs (for customers)

Car Wash Supplies

car air fresheners (page 36)
car made from a cardboard box
bucket
large sponge
squeegee
chamois cloth
toy vacuum cleaner

clean, empty car soap bottle
clean, empty car wax container
clean, empty glass cleaner bottle
roll of paper towels
length of hose with nozzle attached
handled pot scrubber (wheel brush)

Tip!
Attach strips of
blue cellophane (water)
to the hose nozzle.

2. Introduce the theme

♫   **Sparkling Clean**
*(sung to the tune of
"Row, Row, Row Your Boat")*

Spray, spray, spray the car.
Make suds that have a sheen.
Swirl the bubbles all around.
Make it squeaky clean!

3. Suggest several roles

Cashier	Greets customers, asks which services they want, takes/returns car keys, collects payment, issues receipt
Customer	Requests services, pays for services, inspects finished car
Car Washer	Washes and waxes cars, cleans windows, vacuums cars

GLASS CLEANER

4. Inspire plenty of play

● Every few days, suggest a different play scenario, such as the following:
  —Give each customer a free air freshener with his car wash.
  —Offer a full-service wash and wax special for $10.00.
  —Set up a doughnut and coffee bar for customers.

● During group time, ask whether anyone has ever helped wash the family car. If so, have her share what task she performed. Also ask whether anyone has ever been in a car that has gone through an automatic car wash. If so, have her tell about the experience.

Soapy Sam's Car Wash

Note to the teacher: Use with pages 33 and 34. Make a copy of page 36 for your files. Remove this mini poster and put it in a plastic page protector for durability. Then display it at the center at students' eye level.

35

Air Freshener Patterns

Use with pages 33 and 34. Use fruit-scented markers to color a white tagboard copy of the patterns. Cut out the patterns; then punch a hole near the top of each cutout and attach a string for hanging.

apple

TEC61312

strawberry

TEC61312

orange

TEC61312

lemon

TEC61312

Construction Site

1. Choose props

Work Attire and Accessories

hard hat
safety glasses
work gloves
tool belt
painter's hat

Building Supplies

construction zone sign (page 39)
order form (page 40)
blueprints (or draw pretend blueprints)
wooden blocks
oversize linking blocks
foam blocks
toy toolbox with plastic tools
toy tape measure
golf tees (nails to hammer into foam)
toy wheelbarrow or wagon
child-size plastic shovel
chair for work truck (or make a truck from a cardboard box)

PVC pipes and connectors
level
bucket
toy trowel

Painting Supplies

sandpaper
large coffee cans (paint cans, see tip)
paint stir sticks
paint tray
paintbrushes
paint roller

Tip!
Collect empty cans without sharp edges. Wrap each can in a different-color paper; then label the paper with that color's name.

2. Introduce the theme

 Construction Zone by Tana Hoban

 Build It Up
Bang, bang go the hammers
At the construction site.
Floors go down, and walls go up;
It's really quite a sight.

3. Suggest several roles

Construction Site Manager	Oversees work site, checks blueprints, orders building materials
Carpenter	Reads and follows blueprints to build a structure, measures construction materials, saws wood, hammers nails
Brick Mason	Mixes mortar; lays bricks to create foundations, walls, chimneys, and walkways
Plumber	Reads blueprints; connects pipes for a plumbing system; installs sinks, toilets, tubs, and showers
Painter	Sands and prepares surfaces, stirs paint, paints inside or outside of structure

4. Inspire plenty of play

- Every few days, suggest a different play scenario, such as the following:
  - The site manager meets with construction workers to go over blueprints for a skyscraper. When the meeting is over, workers begin the construction project.
  - Construction workers are hard at work building a new school. They are trying to finish construction before the end of summer break.
  - The plans for a new family fitness center are finalized. Construction begins today.

- Encourage each child to draw plans for something he would like to build. Then invite him to share his plans with classmates during group time.

Construction Zone

Hooray for Dramatic Play! ©The Mailbox® Books • TEC61312

Note to the teacher: Use with pages 37 and 38. Make a copy of page 40 for your files. Remove this mini poster and put it in a plastic page protector for durability. Then display it at the center at students' eye level.

Order Form

Item	How Many?
☐ wood	_____
☐ bricks	_____
☐ nails	_____
☐ pipes	_____
☐ paint	_____

Customer's name _____

Note to the teacher: Use with pages 37 and 38. To save paper, laminate one or two copies of this page and provide the same number of wipe-off markers.

Dentist's Office

1. Choose props

Examination Room Supplies

office sign (page 43)
reward certificates (page 44)
dolls (patients)
doll high chair (for dental chair)
copies of dental X-rays
oversize white shirts
dental napkin (see tip)
latex-free exam gloves
small paper cups
unbreakable mirror
toothpaste boxes
new children's toothbrushes
empty floss container
empty mouthwash bottle

pencil
highlighter
file folders
appointment book
telephone
chairs
magazines
basket of toys (for waiting children)

Reception Area

appointment cards (page 44)
desk
clipboard with blank paper (for signing in)

Tip!
To make a dental napkin, tie each end of a length of yarn to separate spring-style clothespins. Then clip the clothespins to an unfolded white or blue paper napkin.

2. Introduce the theme

 Vera Goes to the Dentist by Vera Rosenberry

 Going to the Dentist
(sung to the tune of "The Farmer in the Dell")

I'll go to the dentist.
He'll check my pearly whites.
He'll clean and polish them
To keep them nice and bright!

3. Suggest several roles

Receptionist
Greets patient, asks adult to sign patient in, answers telephone, books and confirms appointments, directs patient to exam room

Adult
Brings patient to office and signs him in, waits with patient in waiting room, accompanies patient to exam room, asks dentist or hygienist questions

Dental Hygienist
Cleans patient's teeth, takes X-rays, assists dentist

Dentist
Examines patient's teeth, looks at X-rays, fills cavities, answers questions

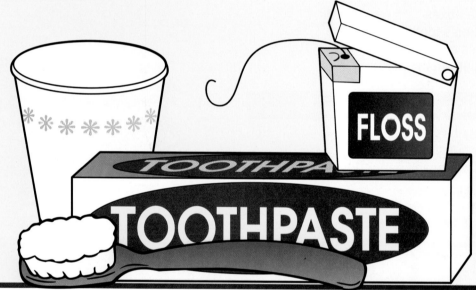

4. Inspire plenty of play

- Every few days, suggest a different play scenario, such as the following:
  — Several six-month checkups are scheduled this week.
  — Dentists who specialize in pain-free cavity treatments are working here this week.
  — A patient has a terrible toothache but won't open her mouth for the dentist to check it. The dentist promises to give her a reward certificate, so she lets him check her tooth. It has a very large cavity that needs to be filled.

- Attach several tooth cutouts to a length of string suspended between two chairs. Demonstrate for youngsters how to floss between the teeth using a length of yarn. Then invite little ones to try!

Healthy Teeth Are Happy Teeth

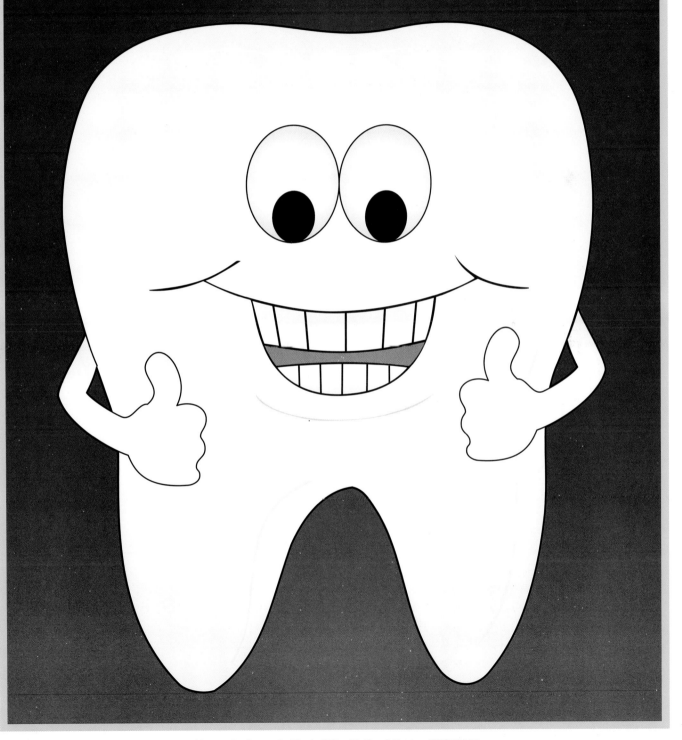

Note to the teacher: Use with pages 41 and 42. Make a copy of page 44 for your files. Remove this mini poster and put it in a plastic page protector for durability. Then display it at the center at students' eye level.

Reward Certificate and Appointment Cards

Use with pages 41 and 42. To save paper, laminate one or two copies of the page and cut apart the certificate and appointment cards. Place the certificates and appointment cards at the center along with wipe-off markers.

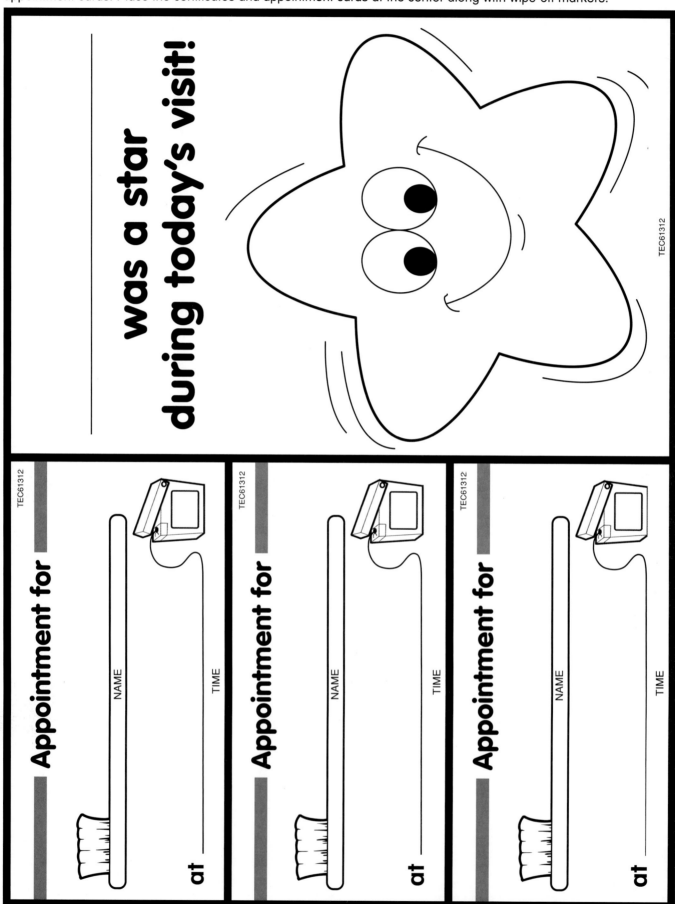

was a star during today's visit!

TEC61312

Appointment for

NAME

at

TIME

TEC61312

Appointment for

NAME

at

TIME

TEC61312

Appointment for

NAME

at

TIME

Doctor's Office

1. Choose props

Examination Supplies

eye chart (page 47)
medical chart (page 48)
dolls (patients)
lab coat or smock
stethoscope
toy thermometer
toy blood pressure cuff
scale for weighing
tongue depressor
cot for patient
pillow
blanket
penlight or small flashlight
clipboard (for doctor to hold)
toy laptop

Treatment Supplies

bandages (cloth or adhesive)
gauze
tongue depressors (for splints)
plastic syringe

ice packs
cotton balls
fabric for making a sling
notepad and pen for writing prescriptions

Office Supplies

clipboard with blank paper (for signing in)
pencil
desk
highlighter
appointment book
file folders
telephone

Waiting Room Supplies

chairs
magazines

Tip!
Ask parents to donate gently used white dress shirts to use as lab coats.

2. Introduce the theme

♪

Doctors Are Helpful
(sung to the tune of "My Bonnie Lies Over the Ocean")

A doctor helps people feel better.
A doctor is someone I see.
A doctor helps people feel better.
Oh, don't take my doctor from me!

3. Suggest several roles

Receptionist	Greets patients, answers telephone, books appointments, confirms appointments, asks patients to sign in, directs patients to waiting room
Adult	Brings patient to the office, signs in patient, waits in waiting room, describes symptoms, asks questions
Doctor	Listens to symptoms, examines and treats patients, answers questions, suggests follow-up appointments
Nurse	Reviews patients' records; takes and records weight, temperature, and blood pressure; helps doctor

4. Inspire plenty of play

- Every few days, suggest a different play scenario, such as the following:
  — The flu season is almost here. Flu shots are free during the next two days.
  — Little ones need to have yearly checkups. Several checkups are scheduled for this week.
  — Doctors who are good at treating breaks and sprains are working in the office this week.
  — Free vision screenings are available today and tomorrow.
  — Suggest possible ailments. For example, touch a doll's forehead and say, "I think this little one has a fever." Or pretend to hear a cough coming from a doll and say, "I think this one needs to see a doctor about her cough."

- Invite a nurse or doctor to visit the classroom. Ask her to show some of the medical tools she uses.

Check Your Vision

Note to the teacher: Use with pages 45 and 46. Make a copy of page 48 for your files. Remove this eye chart and put it in a plastic page protector for durability. Then display it at the center so it can be used when pretending to give eye exams.

Medical Chart

Patient's name _____

Reason for visit

☐ checkup

☐ earache

☐ broken bone

☐ fever

☐ cold/flu

☐ other

Treatment (Check all that apply.)

☐ medicine

☐ shot

☐ bandage

☐ cast

☐ bed rest

☐ other

Doctor _____

Hooray for Dramatic Play! • ©The Mailbox® Books • TEC61312

Note to the teacher: Use with pages 45 and 46. To save paper, laminate one or two copies of this page and provide the same number of wipe-off markers.

Farm

1. Choose props

Farm Clothes

flannel shirts
overalls
straw hats
work boots

Farm Tools and Accessories

plastic child-size pitchfork, rake, shovel, and hoe
buckets
toy toolbox containing plastic tools
toy wheelbarrow or wagon
wooden blocks and boards
bale of hay (check for allergies)
plastic fencing

Livestock Supplies

supersize barn cutout attached to a wall
stuffed toy farm animals
clean, empty food buckets or bags

makeshift chicken coop (see tip)
plastic eggs
basket (for collecting eggs)
brush (for brushing horses)

Crop Supplies

empty seed packets
play produce
bushel baskets
watering can

Tip!
To make a chicken coop, set a cardboard box on its side. Glue brown paper shreds in the box so they resemble a nest. Then add a toy chicken and a few plastic eggs.

2. Introduce the theme

Big Red Barn written by Margaret Wise Brown and illustrated by Felicia Bond

Down at the Farm
(sung to the tune of "The Muffin Man")

Cows and horses, chickens, ewes,
Goats and ducks and piggies too.
They all live in harmony.
It's a farm family!

3. Suggest several roles

Farmer   Plants seeds to grow crops, tends crops, harvests crops, feeds animals, milks cows, gathers eggs, does farm repairs

Farmhand   Assists farmer with daily farm chores

Veterinarian   Helps farm animals when they get sick or hurt

4. Inspire plenty of play

- Every few days suggest a different play scenario, such as the following:
  — The crops are ready for harvesting. The farm workers gather all the crops in one wheelbarrow. Then they sort the fruits and vegetables into separate baskets.
  — Oh no! The gate was left open and the cows got loose! The farmhands round them up and herd them back inside the fence. Then they make sure the gate is locked.
  — The pigs found a perfect place to wallow in the mud. The farmer and the farmhands build a pen around the mud.
  — The farmer goes to the barn to feed the horses, but one refuses to eat. He asks the farmhand to call the veterinarian. The veterinarian comes to the farm, checks the horse, and gives it medicine.

- Play a variation of Duck, Duck, Goose. Substitute farm animal sounds for the animal names. For example, play Moo, Moo, Oink or Baa, Baa, Quack.

Welcome to Friendly Farm

Note to the teacher: Use with pages 49 and 50. Make a copy of page 52 for your files. Remove this mini poster and put it in a plastic page protector for durability. Then display it at the center at students' eye level.

Daily Farm Chores

☐ feed the animals

☐ milk the cows

☐ gather the eggs

☐ brush the horses

☐ clean the barn

☐ take care of crops

Hooray for Dramatic Play! • ©The Mailbox® Books • TEC61312

Note to the teacher: Use with pages 49 and 50. To save paper, laminate one or two copies of this page and provide the same number of wipe-off markers.

Farmers' Market

1. Choose props

Business Supplies

business sign (page 55)
price list (page 56)
money-related props (pages 125–128)
toy cash register

Food Supplies and Accessories

play or real produce
baskets (for produce)
small tables
clean, empty juice bottles
clean, plastic jelly and honey jars
food scale
toy wheelbarrow or wagon
paper grocery bags
paper lunch bags
handheld grocery basket

Customer Supplies

money-related props (pages 125–128)
notepad and pencil (for making a shopping list)
tote bags
pocketbooks
wallets

Tip!
Ask each family to send in a real fruit or vegetable.

2. Introduce the theme

 Market Day by Lois Ehlert

♫ **Crops for Sale**
(sung to the tune of "Head and Shoulders")

Lettuce, peas, tomatoes, tomatoes.
Cabbage, pears, potatoes, potatoes.
Farmers bring their crops to sell.
Farmers' markets sure are swell, sure are swell!

3. Suggest several roles

Farmer — Displays produce and other merchandise, helps customers, weighs produce, sells merchandise, collects payments

Farmer's Assistant — Assists farmer with daily tasks of managing the stand

Customer — Makes shopping list, checks produce, selects desired items, pays for merchandise

4. Inspire plenty of play

- Every few days, suggest a different play scenario, such as the following:
  — Apples are on special this week. Buy one apple and get one free.
  — Tomorrow is the sweet potato pie contest. Customers need help picking out the best sweet potatoes.
  — Homemade jelly and honey are on special today and tomorrow.
  — A local restaurant is offering a new salad bar. The owner visits the market to stock up on everything needed to make great-tasting salads.

- Display several different types of produce. Help youngsters identify each item; then instruct them to close their eyes. Remove an item and place it out of sight. Then ask youngsters to name the missing item.

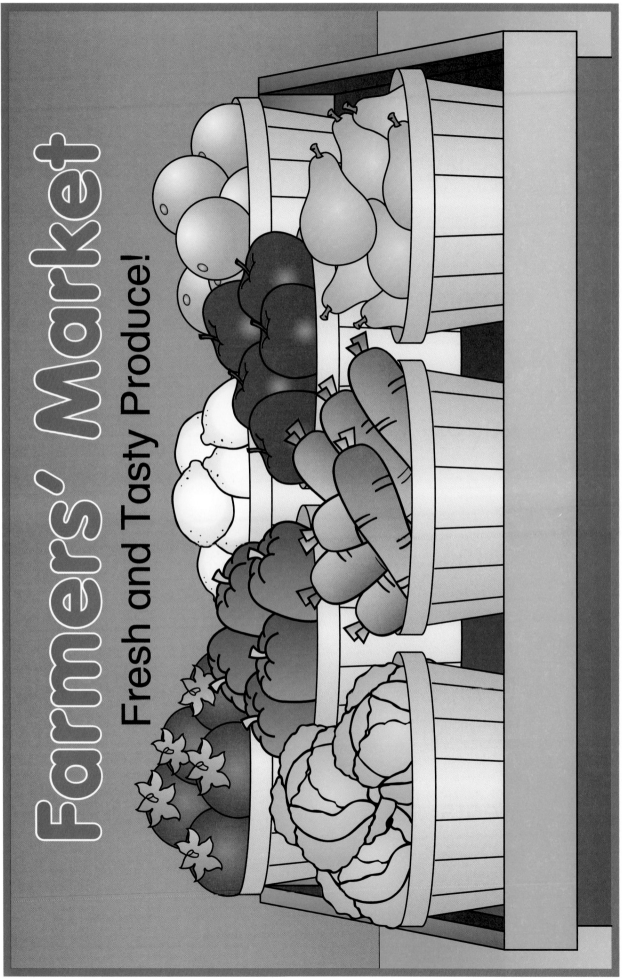

Farmers' Market

Fresh and Tasty Produce!

Hooray for Dramatic Play! • ©The Mailbox® Books • TEC61312

Note to the teacher: Use with pages 53 and 54. Make a copy of page 56 for your files. Remove this mini poster and put it in a plastic page protector for durability. Then display it at the center at students' eye level.

Basket Sale

apples.............................$2.00

potatoes $3.00

carrots $1.00

corn $2.00

peppers $3.00

pears $1.00

Note to the teacher: Use with pages 53 and 54. Place a copy of this page in a plastic sheet protector for durability. Then display it at a center at students' eye level.

Fire Station

1. Choose props

Fire Station Supplies

fire safety sign (page 59)
4 chairs for a fire engine (or make one from a cardboard box)
smoke detector with the wires removed
telephone
notepad and pencil (for writing down information about the fire)
bell
play kitchen appliances
small table and chairs
play dishes, cookware, utensils, and food
books and magazines
bucket and sponge (for cleaning the fire truck)
maps

Firefighting Gear and Accessories

firefighter hats
plastic raincoats
rain boots
gloves
safety goggles
makeshift air tanks (see tip)
walkie-talkies
hose
empty fire extinguisher
flashlights
dolls and stuffed animals (to rescue from burning building)

Tip!
To make an air tank, hot-glue two fabric straps to a clean, empty two-liter bottle. Have a child slip on the air tank as he would a backpack.

2. Introduce the theme

 Fire Engines by Anne Rockwell

A Firefighter's Day
At the fire station,
Firefighters can be found.
They are always ready
When the fire bell sounds.
They'll rush off to the fire,
Spray the flames till they are out.
"Hooray for firefighters!"
They will hear the people shout!

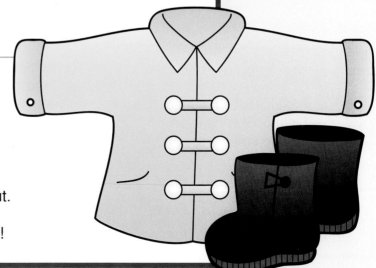

3. Suggest several roles

Fire Chief   Oversees activities at fire station, directs firefighters at fire

Firefighter   Helps people inside burning buildings, extinguishes fires, drives
                     fire engine, washes fire engine, answers telephone, writes down
                     information about location of fire, sounds alarm to alert other
                     firefighters to get ready, teaches youngsters about fire safety

Student   Listens to fire safety rules, asks firefighters questions, answers
                     firefighters' questions, practices fire safety tips

4. Inspire plenty of play

- Every few days, suggest a different play scenario, such as the following:
  — A house is filled with smoke. Firefighters tell the people to stay low and go,
    reminding them to crawl below the smoke so they can find their way out.
  — Firefighters work together to wash the fire truck and repair the equipment before the
    next fire alarm sounds.
  — Little ones visit the fire station to learn about fire safety. The fire chief demonstrates
    how to stop, drop, and roll.

- During group time, invite each child to practice stop, drop, and roll.

- Lead a group discussion about harmful forms of fire (burning building, forest fire) and
  helpful forms of fire (for cooking food, keeping warm, birthday candles).

Note to the teacher: Use with pages 57 and 58. Make a copy of page 60 for your files. Remove this mini poster and put it in a plastic page protector for durability. Then display it at the center at students' eye level.

Badge Patterns

Use with pages 57 and 58. Personalize a tagboard badge cutout for each child and place the badges at the center. When a child visits the center, she finds her badge and tapes it to her shirt.

Hooray for Dramatic Play! • ©The Mailbox® Books • TEC61312

Fitness Center

1. Choose props

Fitness Center Supplies

fitness center sign (page 63)
small table
balance ball
bathroom scale (for weighing)
exercise mats
television with VCR or DVD player
exercise video or DVD for young children
wading pool (whirlpool)
makeshift dumbbells and barbells (see tip)
light hand weights
jump rope
stopwatch
empty spray bottle and clean rag (for cleaning equipment)

Member Supplies

membership cards (page 64)
tote bag or athletic bag
towel
sports bottle
sweatbands for heads and wrists

Tip!
To make a dumbbell or barbell, glue a large tagboard circle to each end of a cardboard tube.

2. Introduce the theme

 From Head to Toe by Eric Carle

 Get Moving
(sung to the tune of "The Farmer in the Dell")

It's time to exercise,
To stretch and reach up high.
To jog and lift some weights.
I love my fitness place!

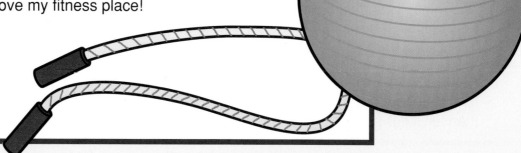

3. Suggest several roles

Fitness Center Employee
Checks members' cards, answers members' questions, keeps fitness center clean, signs up new members

Trainer
Shows members how to use equipment, teaches members how to exercise properly, helps members develop a plan to stay in shape

Fitness Center Member
Shows or scans membership card prior to working out, asks employee and trainer questions, uses equipment to exercise

4. Inspire plenty of play

- Every few days, suggest a different play scenario, such as the following:
  — Prospective members are invited to try out the fitness center free for one week.
  — Dance classes are being offered this week.
  — A fitness trainer schedules a special class to show members how to properly use the dumbbells and barbells.
  — A trainer explains to members that stretching before a workout helps prevent injuries. Then she demonstrates several stretches.

- Conceal in an athletic bag a collection of items, most of which would be used at a fitness center. Invite volunteers, in turn, to take an item from the bag, identify it, and then tell if it is something that would be used at a fitness center.

Fun Times Fitness Center

Open Daily
9:00 AM—9:00 PM

Note to the teacher: Use with pages 61 and 62. Make a copy of page 64 for your files. Remove this mini poster and put it in a plastic page protector for durability. Then display it at the center at students' eye level.

Membership Cards

Use with pages 61 and 62. To save paper, laminate a copy of this page and then cut apart the cards. Put the cards at the center with wipe-off markers.

Fun Times Fitness Center

_____
member's name

TEC61312

Fun Times Fitness Center

_____
member's name

TEC61312

Fun Times Fitness Center

_____
member's name

TEC61312

Fun Times Fitness Center

_____
member's name

TEC61312

Fun Times Fitness Center

_____
member's name

TEC61312

Fun Times Fitness Center

_____
member's name

TEC61312

Flower Shop

1. Choose props

Potted Plant Supplies

tub containing potting soil
plastic scooper
plastic pots
empty seed packets
empty bulb packets
toy gardening tools
watering can
smock
gardening gloves

Floral-Arrangement Supplies

enclosure cards (page 68)
silk flowers
plastic vases
floral foam
tissue paper
cellophane
ribbon
baskets
small toy stuffed animals

Business Supplies

flower shop sign (page 67)
money-related props (pages 125–128)
toy cash register
notepad
pencil
telephone
floral/gardening magazines

Tip!
Ask parents to donate items such as empty seed and bulb packets, plastic pots, vases, and magazines.

2. Introduce the theme

♫ **A Beautiful Arrangement**
(sung to the tune of "Ten Little Indians")

One little, two little, three little roses.
Four little, five little, six little tulips.
Seven little, eight little, nine little daisies.
They're all in a pretty bouquet.

3. Suggest several roles

Florist
Cares for plants; creates floral arrangements; finds out what customers want; answers customers' questions; prepares orders; orders flowers, seeds, bulbs, and floral-arrangement supplies

Florist's Assistant
Greets customers, answers telephone, takes orders, answers questions, delivers flowers, collects payments

Customer
Asks questions, chooses flowers, places order, pays for flowers

4. Inspire plenty of play

- Every few days, suggest a different play scenario such as the following:
  — Roses are on special today and tomorrow. They're $10.00 per dozen!
  — There are many birthday celebrations this week. The florists are busy creating birthday bouquets that each include a small stuffed animal.
  — There is a big, fancy wedding this weekend. The florists are hard at work making the flower arrangements and bridal bouquet.
  — Visit the flower shop today and receive a free flower to give to a friend.
  — Write your name on a paper strip and put it in the "Prize Plant" giveaway box. The lucky winner receives a decorative pot containing a beautiful houseplant!

- Take youngsters on a nature walk to search for different flower types and colors.

Blooms and Blossoms Flower Shop

Note to the teacher: Use with pages 65 and 66. Make a copy of page 68 for your files. Remove this mini poster and put it in a plastic page protector for durability. Then display it at the center at students' eye level.

Enclosure Cards

Use with pages 65 and 66. To save paper, laminate one or two copies of this page and then cut the cards apart. Provide wipe-off markers.

Happy Birthday!

To: _____

From: _____

TEC61312

 # Get Well Soon

To: _____

From: _____

TEC61312

I Miss You

To: _____

From: _____

TEC61312

 # Happy Holidays

To: _____

From: _____

TEC61312

For Someone Special

To: _____

From: _____

TEC61312

Congratulations!

To: _____

From: _____

TEC61312

Hooray for Dramatic Play! • ©The Mailbox® Books • TEC61312

Grocery Store

1. Choose props

Store Supplies

store sign (page 71)
employee nametags (page 72)
money-related props (pages 125–128)
toy cash register
paper grocery bags
toy shopping cart
handheld shopping basket
empty food boxes
clean, empty plastic juice and soda bottles
clean, empty milk jugs
sterilized egg cartons with plastic eggs
play food

Sample-Serving Supplies

latex-free food-service gloves
apron
serving tray

small paper cups
napkins
play food or drink containers (for samples)

Customer Supplies

money-related props
coupon organizer with coupons
grocery store flyers
fabric grocery tote
notepad and pencil (for making a grocery list)

Tip!
Provide coupon inserts from the newspaper for youngsters to cut apart and take to the grocery store.

2. Introduce the theme

 Maisy Goes Shopping by Lucy Cousins

 Going for Groceries
We need bread and milk and more.
Let's go to the grocery store!
Fill the cart with food to eat.
Uh-oh! Don't forget a treat!
Let's be sure to check the list.
Make sure nothing has been missed!

3. Suggest several roles

Store Clerk	Stocks shelves, displays sale signs, assists customers, cleans up spills
Sample Server	Prepares and serves samples, tells customers about product samples
Cashier	Greets customer, answers questions, rings up grocery items, collects payment, gives customer receipt, packs purchases
Customer	Checks sales flyers, writes grocery list, shops for groceries, asks questions if help is needed, uses coupons, pays for purchases

4. Inspire plenty of play

- Every few days, suggest a different play scenario, such as the following:
  — Strawberries are on sale this week. Buy one container and get a second one free!
  — Lots of customers stop by the sample booth to try a new drink called Goo-Goo Juice.
  — Today is double-coupon day! Customers are shopping with coupon organizers filled with coupons.
  — Stormy weather is in the forecast. Customers are rushing to the store to stock up on essential items.

- Conceal several real or play food items in a grocery bag. Provide youngsters with clues to help them guess one of the items. When the item is guessed, remove it from the bag and set it aside. Continue until the bag is empty.

Shop and Save

Hooray for Dramatic Play! • ©The Mailbox® Books • TEC61312

Note to the teacher: Use with pages 69 and 70. Make c copy of page 72 for your files. Remove this mini poster and put it in a plastic page protector for durability. Then display it at the center at students' eye level.

Nametag Patterns

Use with pages 69 and 70. Laminate a copy of this page. Cut apart the nametags and place them at the center with wipe-off markers and tape. Each store employee writes his name on a nametag and then tapes it to his shirt.

Groceries Galore

How may I help you?

TEC61312

Groceries Galore

How may I help you?

TEC61312

Groceries Galore

How may I help you?

TEC61312

Groceries Galore

How may I help you?

TEC61312

Groceries Galore

How may I help you?

TEC61312

Groceries Galore

How may I help you?

TEC61312

Hair Salon

1. Choose props

Salon Supplies

capes
towels
chairs
unbreakable mirror
empty shampoo and conditioner bottles
empty hair dye boxes
latex-free gloves (one pair for each child)
empty spray bottles
child-size broom and dustpan

Styling Supplies

blow-dryer (cord removed)
toy scissors
plastic combs
foam curlers
hair clips
barrettes

Business Supplies

hair-care sign (page 75)
coupons (page 76)
telephone
appointment book
pencils
hairstyle pictures (from magazines or hairstyle
    books)
sign-in sheet
magazines

Tip!
Ask the owner of a local hair salon if she has any outdated hairstyle books she would be willing to donate.

2. Introduce the theme

Snip, Snip!
Welcome to the hair salon!
Short haircut, or keep it long?
To the sink to wash your hair,
Now sit in the styling chair.
Wrap up in a plastic cape.
Now let's get that hair in shape!

3. Suggest several roles

Hairstylist — Asks what customer wants done to hair, covers customer with cape, provides requested hair care—such as wash, cut, color, or blow-dry

Salon Assistant — Assists stylist, washes hair, provides clean capes and towels, sweeps hair off floor

Customer — Makes appointment, checks in with receptionist upon arrival, tells hairstylist what to do, receives hair-care services and advice

Receptionist — Greets customers, answers telephone, books appointments

4. Inspire plenty of play

- Every few days, suggest a different play scenario, such as the following:
  — Offer a Deal of the Day that includes a wash, cut, and blow-dry for $5.00.
  — Give each customer a coupon for $2.00 off her next haircut.
  — A customer comes in with a big wad of gum stuck in her hair. The stylist tries many ways to remove the gum.
  — Several appointments are scheduled this week for customers who are attending a fancy wedding.

- During group time, invite youngsters to share hair-related stories. Ask questions such as the following: Have you ever had a haircut at a real hair salon? Does someone at home cut your hair? Have you ever gotten gum stuck in your hair? If so, how did you get it out?

Hair Care

Shampoo $1.00

Color $10.00

Cut $5.00

Curl $3.00

Blow-Dry $2.00

Note to the teacher: Use with pages 73 and 74. Make a copy of page 76 for your files. Remove this mini poster and put it in a plastic page protector for durability. Then display it at the center at students' eye level.

$2.00 off
Your Next
Haircut!

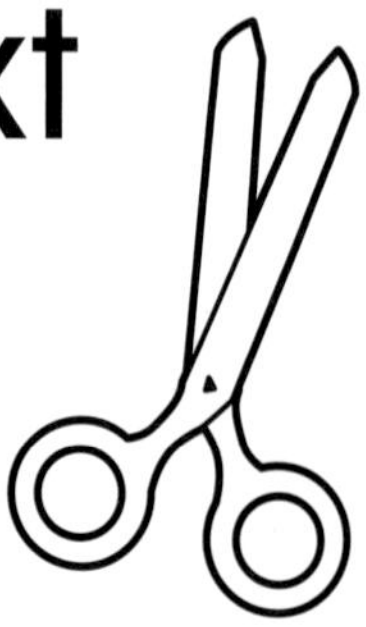

TEC61312

$2.00 off
Your Next
Haircut!

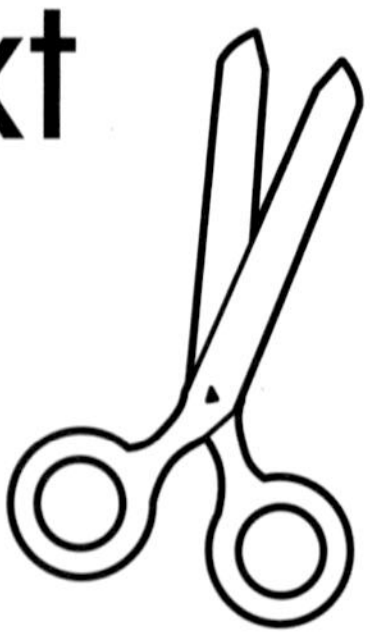

TEC61312

$2.00 off
Your Next
Haircut!

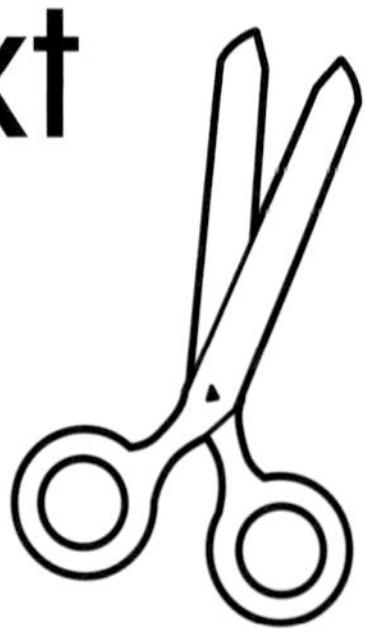

TEC61312

$2.00 off
Your Next
Haircut!

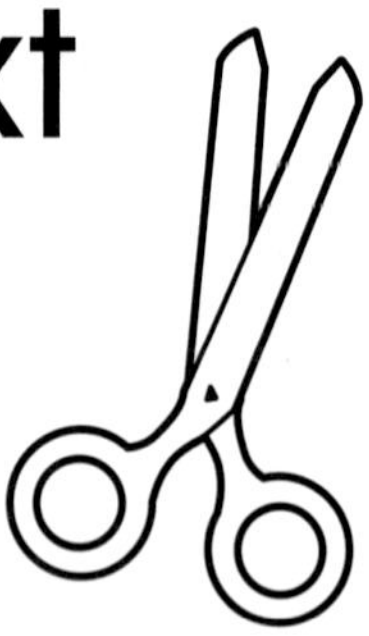

TEC61312

$2.00 off
Your Next
Haircut!

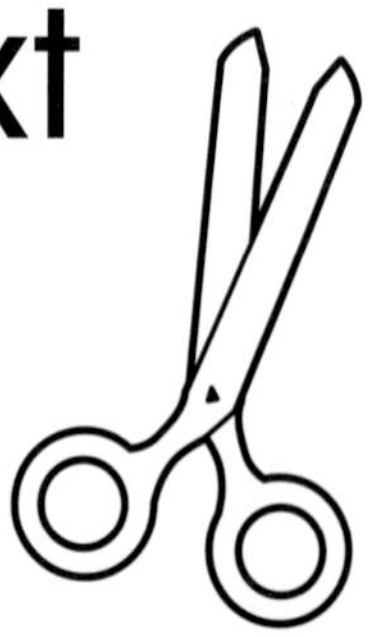

TEC61312

$2.00 off
Your Next
Haircut!

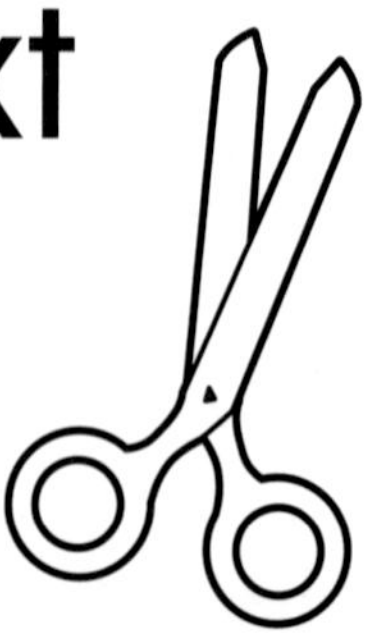

TEC61312

Ice Cream Shop

1. Choose props

Ice Cream Supplies

clean, empty ice cream containers
play dough (ice cream)
brown tagboard cones or disposable cups

Topping Supplies

empty candy-sprinkle container
clean, empty plastic ice cream topping
    bottles
empty whipped cream can or container
plastic fruit, such as bananas and
    strawberries
red pom-poms (cherries)

Preparation Supplies

disposable bowls
ice cream scoop
plastic knife (for "slicing" fruit)
tongs (for picking up fruit)
spoons

Business Supplies

ice cream shop sign (page 79)
order sheet (page 80)
money-related props (pages 125–128)
toy cash register
latex-free food-service gloves (one pair for
    each child)
napkins

Tip!
Ask parents to donate
clean, empty ice cream
containers and topping
bottles.

2. Introduce the theme

Curious George Goes to an Ice Cream Shop by
Margret and H. A. Rey

Frosty Treats
Ice cream sundae, cone, or shake:
What would you like me to make?
I'll scoop ice cream for your treat.
Cold and tasty! Oh so sweet!
Pay me for your treat and then
I'll say, "Thanks! Please come again!"

3. Suggest several roles

Customer Chooses type of treat, ice cream flavor(s), and desired topping(s); gives order to server; pays for order; eats treat

Server Greets customers, takes orders, brings orders to scooper, delivers orders to customers, collects payments

Scooper Reads and fills orders, passes treats to server

4. Inspire plenty of play

- Vary the selection of pretend ice cream toppings.

- Every few days, suggest a different play scenario, such as the following:
  — A two-day special featuring a triple-scoop sundae topped with melted marshmallows, bananas, and mint chocolate chips
  — An ice cream buffet where customers order ice cream treats (without toppings) and then garnish them as desired
  — A friends and family event where customers buy one ice cream and get a second one free

- Give each child a personal invitation to an ice cream social. Set out items needed for making real ice cream sundaes. When the guests are settled in, have each child place her order and have adults act as scoopers and servers.

Frosty Treats

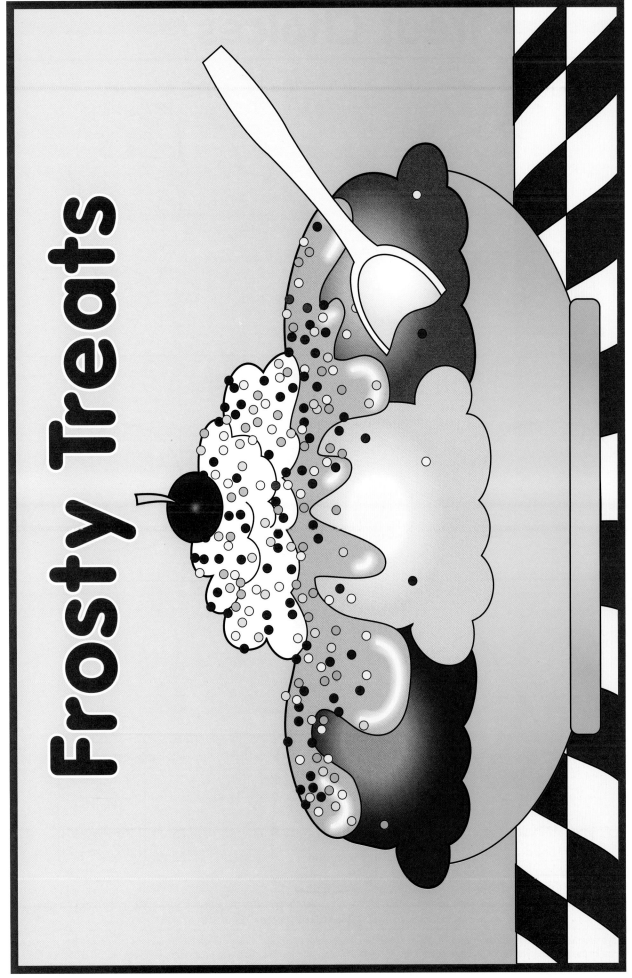

Hooray for Dramatic Play! • ©The Mailbox® Books • TEC61312

Note to the teacher: Use with pages 77 and 78. Make a copy of page 80 for your files. Remove this mini poster and put it in a plastic page protector for durability. Then display it at the center at students' eye level.

Treat Choices

☐ Sundae   ☐ Cone

Ice Cream Flavors

☐   ☐   ☐

Toppings

☐ Whipped Cream   ☐ Squeeze Topping   ☐ Sprinkles

Hooray for Dramatic Play! • ©The Mailbox® Books • TEC61312

Note to the teacher: Use with pages 77 and 78. Make two or three copies of this page. Color the ice cream scoops to indicate flavor choices and the rest of the page as you like. Laminate each page and provide wipe-off markers. To place an order, a child checks off a desired treat, ice cream flavor(s), and topping(s).

Movie Theater

1. Choose props

Concession Stand Supplies

concession stand menu (page 83)
money-related props (pages 125–128)
toy cash register
popcorn buckets or bags (see tip)
disposable drink cups
laminated snack wrappers
empty candy boxes
napkins

Ticket Booth Supplies

movie tickets (page 84)
money-related props (pages 125–128)
toy cash register or money tray

Theater Supplies

white bulletin board paper (movie screen)
movie posters (for display and posting on
    movie screen)
overhead projector
3-D glasses or sunglasses
chairs

Cleaning Supplies

broom
dustpan

Tip!
For an authentic scent,
stuff empty microwave popcorn
bags with paper and staple
the openings closed!

2. Introduce the theme

♫

Let's Go to the Movies
(sung to the tune of "My Bonnie Lies Over the Ocean")

Would you like to go to the movies?
We'll each buy a ticket, and then
We'll get snacks and sit in the theater
And wait for the film to begin.
Movies, movies! So many good movies to see, to see!
Movies, movies! Please come to the movies with me!

3. Suggest several roles

Ticket Booth Attendant	Greets moviegoers, asks what movie they want to see, gives out movie tickets, collects payments
Moviegoer	Asks ticket booth attendant for desired ticket, pays for ticket, buys treats at concession stand, gives ticket to usher, goes in theater, finds seat
Usher	Takes moviegoers' tickets and admits them to theater, helps clean theater
Concession Stand Clerk	Takes food and drink orders, hands out orders, collects payments

4. Inspire plenty of play

● Periodically mount a different poster on the movie screen to add variety.

● Every few days, suggest a different play scenario, such as the following:
  —A new 3-D movie starts today. Moviegoers pick up 3-D glasses at the ticket booth so they can see the special movie effects.
  —There's a children's movie special today and tomorrow. See two movies for the price of one!
  —A concession stand special is popcorn and a drink for $3.00!

● Invite students to draw pictures of their favorite movie characters to share during group time.

Sweet and Salty Snacks

 Popcorn $4.00

 Peanuts $3.00

 Pretzels................ $2.00

 Candy $2.00

 Soda $1.00

Outer Space

1. Choose props

Outer Space Supplies

black bulletin board paper (mount in area for space background)
self-adhesive stars (attach to black paper)
tagboard moon and planets (suspend from ceiling)

Spaceship Supplies

markers and clipboard with observation sheet (page 88)
large appliance box (cut out door and window; cover box with foil)
milk caps and jar lids (hot-glue in box for control panel)
flashlights
toy walkie-talkies
individual play food in resealable plastic bags
chairs
magnifying glasses

Spacesuit Supplies

stuffed backpack (oxygen tank)
toy helmet or bike helmet
oversize gray sweatshirt
heavy work gloves
boots
goggles

Command Post Supplies

countdown poster (page 87)
table and chairs
old computer monitor (or one made from a cardboard box)
old keyboard
headphones
telephone
notepads and pencils
space-related books and magazines

Tip!
Visit a local appliance vendor and ask for a refrigerator box.

2. Introduce the theme

 I Want to Be an Astronaut by Byron Barton

♪ **Soaring Through Space**
(sung to the tune of "Twinkle, Twinkle, Little Star")

Astronauts dress in spacesuits,
And they wear magnetic boots.
On a shuttle, off they race,
Blasting into outer space.
Soaring through the brilliant stars,
Maybe they will land on Mars!

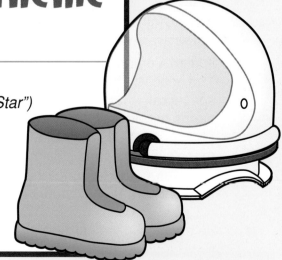

3. Suggest several roles

Astronaut
Gets medical checkup prior to mission, puts on spacesuit, boards spacecraft, works spacecraft control panel, communicates with command post, takes notes on space observations

Command Post Technician
Communicates with astronauts, uses computer to monitor space mission, records important information

Doctor
Examines astronauts prior to mission, travels on spacecraft

4. Inspire plenty of play

● Provide materials—such as Bubble Wrap cushioning material or foam—for youngsters to walk on (moon's surface). Also provide medium-size rocks (moon rocks).

● Every few days, suggest a different play scenario, such as the following:
— There are strange objects flying all around the spacecraft as it zooms through outer space! Contact the command post to tell them what's happening!
— The spacecraft lands on an unknown planet. As the astronauts prepare to leave the spacecraft, they hear a knock on the door! What happens when a crew member opens the door?
— The spaceship lands safely on the moon. The astronauts go outside, investigate the moon's surface, and collect moon rocks to bring back to Earth.
— On a return trip to Earth, the astronauts hear a strange sound coming from inside the spacecraft! They cautiously search to find out what it is.

● Invite each child to share his space adventure observation sheet during group time.

10, 9, 8, 7, 6, 5, 4, 3, 2, 1, Blast Off!

Hooray for Dramatic Play! • ©The Mailbox® Books • TEC61312

Note to the teacher: Use with pages 85 and 86. Make a copy of page 88 for your files. Remove this mini poster and put it in a plastic page protector for durability. Then display it at the center at students' eye level.

87

Space Journey
Observation Sheet

Date _____

by _____

Note to the teacher: Use with pages 85 and 86. Provide a supply of copies of this page. Encourage youngsters to draw or write about something that happens during their pretend space journey.

Pet Store

1. Choose props

Pets and Accessories

toy animals
pet collars
leashes
pet toys
doll clothes (dog clothing)
pet bedding (see tip)
pet carrier or cardboard box

Food and Habitat Supplies

clean, empty pet food containers and bags
plastic pet food dishes
plastic fish bowl
clean pet cage
clear plastic pet container
brown paper shreds (small pet bedding)

Grooming Supplies

product labels (page 92)
clean, empty shampoo-type bottles
clean, empty plastic shaker containers
clean, empty spray bottles
brushes
combs

Business Supplies

business sign (page 91)
money-related props (pages 125–128)
cash register
paper shopping bags
pet-related magazines, pamphlets, and
    coupons
shopping cart or basket

Tip!
For cat or dog bedding, slip a pillow into a decorative pillowcase.

2. Introduce the theme

🎵

At the Pet Store
(sung to the tune of "Did You Ever See a Lassie?")

Oh, we're working at the pet store
With puppies and kittens.
Oh, we're working at the pet store
With rabbits and mice.
We feed them and brush them
And pet them and love them.
Oh, we're working at the pet store.
This job is so nice!

3. Suggest several roles

Cashier Greets customers, rings up products on cash register, puts products in shopping bags, collects payments

Sales Associate Answers customers' questions about pets and pet-related products, helps take care of animals, helps tidy store

Customer Visits store to buy pet or pet-related products, asks sales associate questions, takes pet or pet-related products to cashier, pays for products

4. Inspire plenty of play

● Periodically add a new pet or pet-related product to the store.

● Every few days, suggest a different play scenario, such as the following:
— Have a pet adoption day. Encourage customers to give loving homes to pets in need.
— Arrange for doggy play dates at the store. Customers bring their dogs for fun and exercise with other friendly pooches. (Written proof of vaccinations is required.)
— Offer a free pet food and treats buffet. Invite customers to bring a pet to the store to try some tasty samples.
— Hold a cutest pet contest. The winner gets a basket of pet treats and toys!

● During group time, invite youngsters to share pet store experiences and photos of a family pet bought at a pet store.

"Paws-itively" Pets

Hooray for Dramatic Play! • ©The Mailbox® Books • TEC61312

Note to the teacher: Use with pages 89 and 90. Make c copy of page 92 for your files. Remove this mini poster and put it in a plastic page protector for durability. Then display it at the center at students' eye level.

Pet Product Labels

Use with pages 89 and 90. Copy and cut out the labels. Attach each label to a container to match the grooming supplies list on page 89.

Fabulous Fur
Powder for Sensitive Skin

No More Pests!
Flea and Tick Powder

Fabulous Fur
Clean-Scent Spray

No More Pests!
Flea and Tick Spray

Fabulous Fur
Soft and Shiny Shampoo

No More Pests!
Flea and Tick Shampoo

Pizza Take-Out and Delivery

1. Choose props

Food Supplies

tan felt circles (pizza crusts)
slightly smaller red felt circles (sauce)
felt in various shapes and colors
   (pizza toppings)
empty plastic seasoning jars

Kitchen Supplies

ladle
saucepan
large plastic mixing bowl
measuring cups and spoons
rolling pin
pizza pan
plastic pizza cutter
pizza slice server
oven mitts
aprons
chef's hat
latex-free food service gloves (one pair for
   each child)

pizza peel (cardboard circle with a paint stick
   attached)
play oven

Business Supplies

pizza shop sign (page 95)
toppings menu (page 96)
money-related props (pages 125–128)
toy cash register
telephones (for the pizza shop and customers
   who call for delivery)
notepad and pencil (for taking orders)
clean, empty pizza boxes

Delivery Supplies

chair for pizza delivery car
   (or make a car from a
   cardboard box)

Tip!
Ask the owner of a
local pizzeria to donate
a few unused pizza
boxes.

2. Introduce the theme

Pizza at Sally's by Monica Wellington

Pizza, Please!
Roll out the dough; then give it a toss.
When it's flat, add pizza sauce!
Sprinkle on some tasty cheese.
Add mushrooms and pepperoni, please!
Put the pizza in the oven to bake.
How many minutes will it take?
Slice the pizza; it's time to eat.
This tasty pizza can't be beat!

3. Suggest several roles

Customer   Places order by visiting pizza shop or calling for delivery, chooses desired toppings, pays for pizza at shop or upon delivery

Server   Greets customers, answers telephone, writes down customers' orders, passes orders to chef, gives pizza to customers, collects customers' payments

Chef   Reads orders, makes pizzas, puts pizzas in pizza boxes, slices pizzas with pizza cutter

Delivery Person   Puts pizza in delivery car, "drives" to designated location, gives pizza to customer, collects customer's money, drives to next destination or back to pizza shop

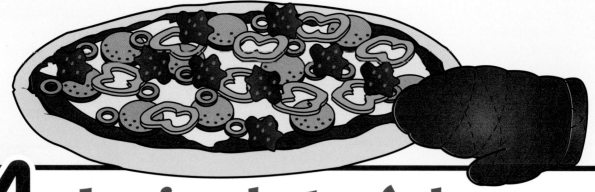

4. Inspire plenty of play

- Every few days, suggest a different play scenario, such as the following:
  — Offer a take-out special! Sell one large pizza with a topping of the customer's choice for only $5.00!
  — When a customer calls to place an order, his delivery is free when he says, "Peppy's Pizza is the best!"
  — Have a pizza raffle! A customer writes his name on a slip of paper and drops it in a raffle box. The lucky customer whose name is drawn gets one free large pizza!
  — Hold a Create Your Own Pizza Day! Jazz up your pizza with any of the unique toppings at the pizza-toppings buffet!

- During group time, invite students to tell what their favorite pizza toppings are and then have them describe the best pizzas they've ever eaten.

Peppy's Pizza

Take-Out and Delivery

Note to the teacher: Use with pages 93 and 94. Make a copy of page 96 for your files. Remove this mini poster and put it in a plastic page protector for durability. Then display it at the center at students' eye level.

Tasty Toppings!

 Mushrooms

 Peppers

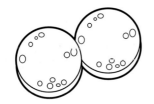 Pepperoni

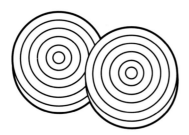 Onions

 Olives

Hooray for Dramatic Play! • ©The Mailbox® Books • TEC61312

Note to the teacher: Use with pages 93 and 94. To save paper, laminate several copies of this page and provide wipe-off markers. Before placing an order, a child circles the pictures of her desired toppings.

Police Station

1. Choose props

Station Supplies

911 sign (page 99)
toy walkie-talkies
telephone
notepads and pencils
table and chairs
computer keyboard

Uniform Supplies

police hats and badges (page 100)
light-blue shirts
toy handcuffs
rain ponchos (for use when on foot patrol
   during a storm)

Patrol Supplies

chair for police car (or make a car from
   a cardboard box)
flashlights
toy megaphone
handheld stop/go traffic sign
memo pad and pencil (for writing tickets)
bicycle horn (attach to police car for
   siren)
safety cones

Tip!
Check a local dollar store
for police-related toys!

2. Introduce the theme

♫
Police Patrol
(sung to the tune of "Pop! Goes the Weasel")

All around the neighborhood
Police are on patrol.
They are there to give us help.
That is their goal.

3. Suggest several roles

Police Dispatcher/911 Operator	Answers telephone, gathers information, determines whether situation is emergency or nonemergency, relays information to appropriate responders
Patrol Officer	Observes neighborhood, keeps citizens safe, helps people solve problems, directs traffic, writes tickets, makes arrests when necessary
Police Detective	Gathers information, investigates clues to solve crimes

4. Inspire plenty of play

- Every few days, suggest a different play scenario, such as the following:
  - Pedestrian traffic is heavy near the blocks and the housekeeping area. An officer is dispatched with a stop/go traffic sign to manage the flow of traffic.
  - Two citizens are engaged in a dispute over a toy. A police officer is dispatched to the scene to help solve the problem.
  - An officer is dispatched to the scene of a minor car accident. He checks to see whether everyone is okay, asks the drivers and eyewitnesses questions about the accident, and then writes a report (and tickets if necessary) using the information.
  - A popular classroom toy has disappeared! A police detective questions classroom members, writes down important information, and then investigates to determine what happened to the toy.

- Help each child learn her full name and address. Using a toy telephone, have each youngster practice making a 911 call. Discuss situations when it is appropriate to call 911 and when it is not.

In an Emergency
Call 911

Note to the teacher: Use with pages 97 and 98. Make a copy of page 100 for your files. Remove this mini poster and put it in a plastic page protector for durability. Then display it at the center at students' eye level.

Police Hat and Badge Patterns

Use with pages 97 and 98. Color and cut out a copy of the patterns. (Laminate the badges for durability.) Glue the hat to a 3" by 18" tagboard strip; then attach self-adhesive Velcro fasteners to each end of the strip to make an adjustable headband.

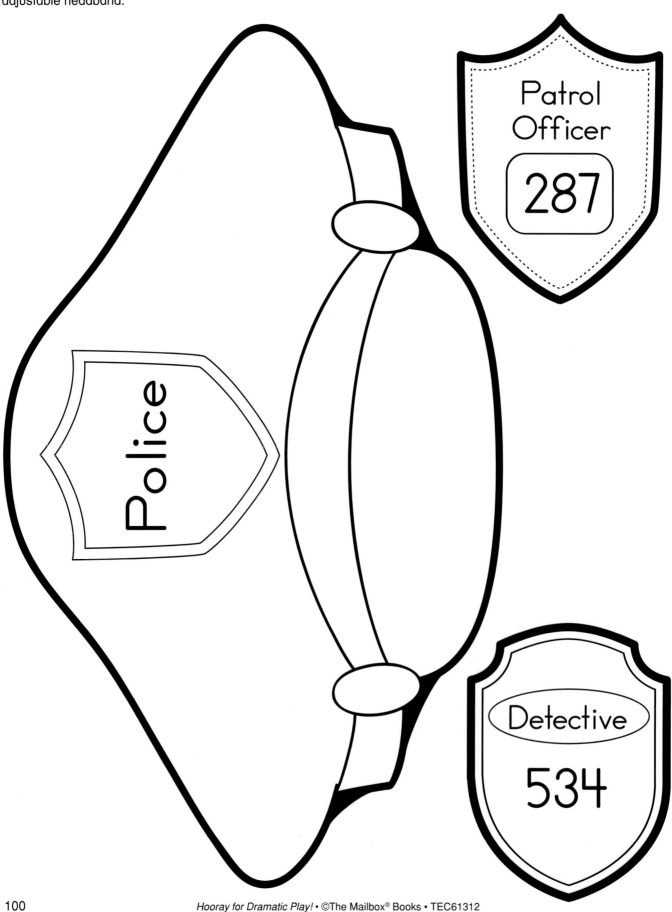

Hooray for Dramatic Play! ©The Mailbox® Books • TEC61312

Post Office

1. Choose props

Post Office Supplies

post office sign (page 103)
money-related props (pages 125–128)
toy cash register
makeshift mailbox
light blue shirt (for postal uniform)
scale (for weighing envelopes and packages)
canceled postage stamps, promotional stamps, stickers
stampers and ink pads
baskets (for sorting mail)
small booklets (for stamp collecting and passports)
toy camera (for taking passport photos)
markers
tape

Mail Supplies

address labels (page 104)
boxes in varying sizes

Bubble Wrap cushioning material
assortment of envelopes
magazines, catalogs, junk mail
student mailboxes (made from shoeboxes or shoe bag)

Mail Carrier Supplies

chair for mail truck (or make a truck from a cardboard box)
tote bag (for mailbag)
outerwear for inclement weather, such as a rain poncho and rubber boots

Tip!
Ask parents to donate canceled stamps and used Priority Mail envelopes and boxes.

2. Introduce the theme

 Delivering Your Mail written by Ann Owen and illustrated by Eric Thomas

 All Kinds of Mail
Postal workers deliver the mail
Come rain, sleet, snow, or hail.
Letters, cards, and packages too
For people just like me and you!

3. Suggest several roles

Postal Clerk	Greets customers, answers questions, sorts mail, weighs packages, calculates postage, sells stamps and other postal products, collects payments
Mail Carrier	Carries mailbag or drives mail truck, follows route to deliver mail
Customer	Buys stamps and other postal products, picks up or mails letters and packages, applies for passport and has passport photo taken

4. Inspire plenty of play

- Provide an assortment of items to pack in shipping boxes.

- Every few days, suggest a different play scenario, such as the following:
  — Today is pen pal day! Classroom pen pals are busy drawing pictures and writing letters to each other.
  — It's raining cats and dogs! Mail carriers bundle up in rain gear to deliver the mail.
  — The post office is bustling with people getting passport photos taken for upcoming vacations.
  — Stamp collectors visit the post office to purchase stamps from a unique "Stamp Collector's Display!"

- Ask each parent to send in an unused postage stamp. Encourage each child to draw a picture for his family and then dictate or write a message; then help him ready it for the mail. Youngsters and their families will be delighted when their special delivery arrives!

STAMPS

book of stamps

roll of stamps

single stamp

U.S. Post Office

U.S. Mail

Note to the teacher: Use with pages 101 and 102. Make a copy of page 104 for your files. Remove this mini poster and put it in a plastic page protector for durability. Then display it at the center at students' eye level.

Address Labels

Use with pages 101 and 102. Make several copies of this page. To save paper, cut out and laminate each label and supply wipe-off markers. If desired, provide student names and addresses for youngsters to copy onto the labels.

Mail

_____
(name)

_____
(street)

_____
(town)

_____
(zip code)

TEC61312

Mail

_____
(name)

_____
(street)

_____
(town)

_____
(zip code)

TEC61312

Hooray for Dramatic Play! • ©The Mailbox® Books • TEC61312

Restaurant

1. Choose props

Business Supplies

restaurant sign (page 107)
menu (page 108)
money-related props (pages 125–128)
notepads and pencils (for taking orders)
toy cash register

Dining Supplies

tablecloth
square napkins (see tip)
tableware
plastic salt and pepper shakers
clean, empty condiment squeeze bottles

Kitchen Supplies

play food
pots and pans
cooking utensils
aprons
oven mitts
chef's hat
trays
dinnerware

Tip!
Fold the napkins into different shapes and sizes, such as large and small rectangles, triangles, and squares.

2. Introduce the theme

 Froggy Eats Out written by Jonathan London and illustrated by Frank Remkiewicz

 Let's Eat Out!
Welcome to the restaurant.
Come in and have a seat.
Look over our menu.
What would you like to eat?
Have a glass of water
And bread while you wait.
Now I'll serve your food.
It sure tastes great!

3. Suggest several roles

Host or Hostess	Makes reservations, greets customers, leads customers to their table
Waiter or Waitress	Provides menus, writes down customers' food and drink orders, passes food orders to chef, brings food and drinks to customers, checks on customers during meal, gives customers meal check, collects payment
Customer	Looks at menu, places food and drink order, eats meal, asks waiter or waitress to bring the check, pays for meal
Chef	Reads customers' orders, cooks food

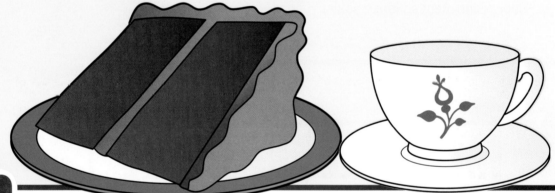

4. Inspire plenty of play

- Periodically offer food items not listed on the regular menu to use as specials.

- Every few days, suggest a different play scenario, such as the following:
  — Feature a "Make It Your Way Salad Buffet" today and tomorrow for only $2.00 per person.
  — Sample the chef's surprise dish! Guess the secret ingredient (three clues provided), and your meal is free!
  — Offer a dining and dancing event featuring the most popular musical hits.
  — Prior to the activity, circle desired letters on the menu. Students correctly name the circled letters to win a free dessert.

- During group time, invite each child to tell about a restaurant where she likes to eat. List the name of each eatery; then help youngsters determine if there is a class favorite.

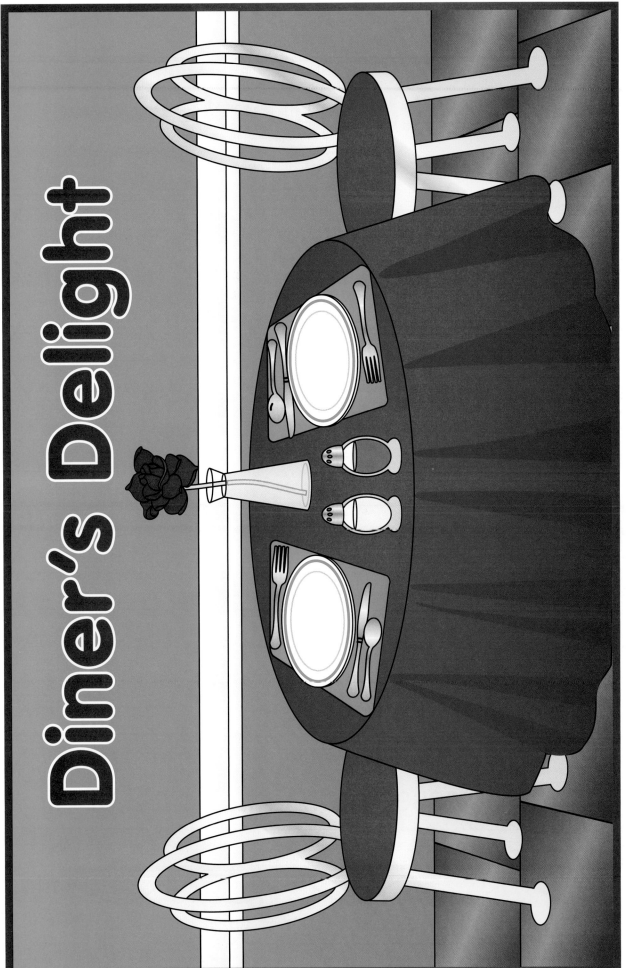

Diner's Delight

Hooray for Dramatic Play! • ©The Mailbox® Books • TEC61312

Note to the teacher: Use with pages 105 and 106. Make a copy of page 108 for your files. Remove this mini poster and put it in a plastic page protector for durability. Then display it at the center at students' eye level.

Lunch Specials

Hamburger $3.00

Chicken $4.00

French Fries $2.00

Corn $1.00

Carrots $1.00

Sandwich $2.00

Chef's Surprise $5.00

Dessert $2.00

Note to the teacher: Use with pages 105 and 106. (See "Inspire plenty of play" for a letter-identification scenario.) To save paper, laminate several copies of this page.

School

1. Choose props

Classroom Supplies

welcome sign (page 111)
attendance sheet (page 112)
desk or small table
chairs
carpet squares (for circle time)
chalkboard or whiteboard
chalk or wipe-off markers
board eraser
small pointer
small bell

School Supplies

notebooks
paper
writing tools

storybooks
puzzles
puppets
toys
musical instruments
paper plates and cups (for pretend snack)

Student Supplies

name cards
backpacks
lunch sacks containing play food

Tip!
Ask family members or friends with children to donate spare backpacks.

2. Introduce the theme

 Off to School, Baby Duck! written by Amy Hest and illustrated by Jill Barton

School Is Fun
(sung to the tune of "Did You Ever See a Lassie?")

It's fun to go to school, to school, to school.
It's fun to go to school to learn with our friends.
We'll sing songs and read books.
We'll eat snacks and play games.
It's fun to go to school to learn with our friends!

3. Suggest roles

Teacher Greets students, directs them to sign attendance sheet, conducts circle time, reads stories, asks and answers questions, sings songs, hands out snack, calls parent if child is sick, writes parent notes

Teacher Assistant Assists teacher with classroom activities and duties

Student Greets teacher, puts backpack away, writes name on attendance sheet, engages in classroom activities, eats snack or lunch, packs backpack to go home

4. Inspire plenty of play

- Periodically change the play materials and books.

- Every few days, suggest a different play scenario, such as the following:
  — A music teacher leads students in singing songs and playing instruments.
  — A storyteller with puppets visits the class and tells youngsters a story.
  — A nature specialist brings animals (toy or stuffed) to the classroom for youngsters to learn about. She reminds students to wash their hands after touching the animals.

- During group time, invite youngsters to tell something they would change about the real classroom or do differently if they were the teacher. With safety in mind, try a few of the ideas to see what happens!

Hooray for Dramatic Play! • ©The Mailbox® Books • TEC61312

Note to the teacher: Use with pages 109 and 110. Make a copy of page 112 for your files. Remove this mini poster and put it in a plastic page protector for durability. Then display it at the center at students' eye level.

111

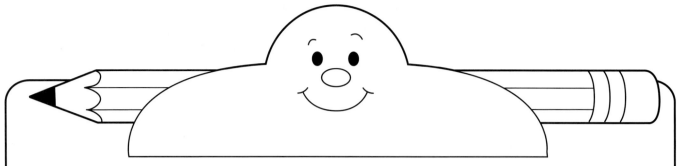

Who Is Here Today?

Name _____

Name _____

Name _____

Name _____

Name _____

Name _____

Hooray for Dramatic Play! • ©The Mailbox® Books • TEC61312

Note to the teacher: Use with pages 109 and 110. To save paper, laminate a copy of this page and provide a wipe-off marker.

Sports Shop

1. Choose props

General Store Supplies

store sign (page 115)
merchandise tags (page 116)
money-related props (pages 125–128)
toy cash register
blank paper and markers (for making signs)
plastic shelves
table
paper grocery bags
sports catalogs

Sports Merchandise

assortment of balls
safety gear, such as knee pads and shin
   guards
plastic baseball bat
baseball mitt
plastic golf clubs
toy bowling ball and pins
goggles
exercise mat

exercise video or DVD
makeshift dumbbells and barbells (See
   fitness center tip on page 61.)
toy fishing pole
tackle box
sports magazines
tote bags (gym bags)
reusable water bottles

Clothing Merchandise

T-shirts
shorts
tennis shoes
sports team clothing
baseball caps

Tip!
Ask parents and coworkers to donate clean, gently used sports-related items, such as clothing and tennis shoes.

2. Introduce the theme

♫ **Working at the Sports Shop**
(sung to the tune of
"I've Been Working on the Railroad")

I've been working at the sports shop
All through the day.
I've been helping people find things
For the sports they like to play.
Shoes and balls and sports equipment—
The things that they will need.
They can find them at the sports shop.
Oh yes, they can indeed!

3. Suggest roles

Store Clerk Orders merchandise, stocks merchandise displays, greets customers, assists customers, answers questions about merchandise

Customer Looks at store merchandise, asks questions, chooses items to purchase, pays for merchandise

Cashier Greets customers, rings up and bags customers' purchases, collects payment

4. Inspire plenty of play

- Every few days, suggest a different play scenario such as the following:
  — All baseball merchandise is on sale today and tomorrow.
  — Buy one sports or exercise DVD and get a second one free!
  — Receive a free sports water bottle with any $5.00 purchase.
  — The big clearance sale starts today. Store clerks are busy tagging clearance items.
  — A celebrity athlete will visit the store today to sign autographs!
  — Sign up for our sports clinic. Watch demonstrations on properly holding a baseball bat, a golf club, a football, and more!

- During group time, invite youngsters to share about sports they like to play or watch.

On the Move
Sports Shop

Hooray for Dramatic Play! ©The Mailbox® Books • TEC61312

Note to the teacher: Use with pages 113 and 114. Make a copy of page 116 for your files. Remove this mini poster and put it in a plastic page protector for durability. Then display it at the center at students' eye level.

Merchandise Tags

Use with pages 113 and 114. Cut out several copies of the tags and laminate them. Then place them at the center with wipe-off markers and tape.

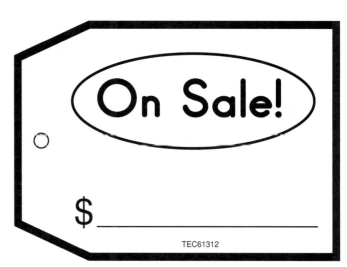

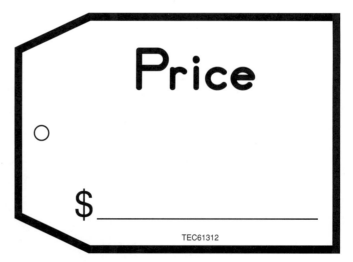

TV Station

1. Choose props

Studio Supplies

studio sign (page 119)
clamp light (studio light)
toy microphone
table and chairs (for news anchors)
director's chair
toy camcorder or TV camera (see tip)
headphones

Program Supplies

weather cards (page 120)
large map (for posting weather cards to do weather report)
magazine pictures (for news stories and commercial advertising)
whiteboard (for posting magazine pictures and map)
large cardboard-box TV (for *Puppet Play* scenario)

assorted puppets
mat and music player (for *Aerobicize* scenario)

Makeup and Wardrobe Supplies

makeup brushes
empty containers (for pretend makeup)
combs
dress-up clothes, including outerwear for roving reporters

Tip!

To make a TV camera, hot-glue the bottom of a disposable cup (camera lens) to one end of a cardboard box and then add desired details.

2. Introduce the theme

At the TV Station

A TV station has reporters
Who tell the news each day.
They broadcast sports and weather.
There's so much they have to say!
So turn on your TV set
And tune in to the news
Or watch your favorite program.
It's up to you to choose!

3. Suggest several roles

TV Director Selects, plans, and schedules programs; supervises stage crew and operations such as cameras, props, microphones, and lighting

TV Personality Performs professional role, such as newscaster, reporter, weatherperson, TV show host, actor, or commercial advertiser

TV Crew Member Specializes in hair and makeup, camera operation, lighting, or managing stage props

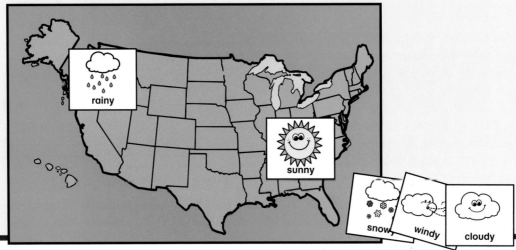

4. Inspire plenty of play

- Vary the magazine pictures to inspire descriptive language and creative broadcasting and advertising.

- Every few days, suggest a different play scenario, such as the following:
  — A meteorologist does an outdoor weather forecast during a windy rainstorm. Inside the station, a check of the local weather map shows rain and high winds for the next two days.
  — The TV station interrupts regular broadcasting with breaking news from a roving reporter. She reports that a bear climbed a tree near a local grocery store and that police officers are on the scene trying to coax the bear down.
  — Broadcast *Puppet Play,* a prime-time special for viewers of all ages!
  — A new show called *Aerobicize,* an exercise program that's fun for all ages, airs today.

- During group time, invite volunteers (reporters) to use the microphone and role-play interviews with classmates (local citizens).

Little Learners TV Station

Director

Breaking News!

Breaking
News!
by
Ms. Robinson's Class

Hooray for Dramatic Play! • ©The Mailbox® Books • TEC61312

Note to the teacher: Use with pages 117 and 118. Make a copy of page 120 for your files. Remove this mini poster and put it in a plastic page protector for durability. Then display it at the center at students' eye level.

Weather Cards

Use with pages 117 and 118. Color a copy of this page as desired. Cut out the cards and laminate them for durability.

sunny
TEC61312

cloudy
TEC61312

rainy
TEC61312

snowy
TEC61312

windy
TEC61312

foggy
TEC61312

Hooray for Dramatic Play! • ©The Mailbox® Books • TEC61312

Veterinary Clinic

1. Choose props

Patients and Accessories

stuffed animals
pet collars
leashes
cardboard pet carrier or box

Examination Supplies

lab coat or smock
stethoscope
magnifying glass
flashlight
scale for weighing
tongue depressor

Treatment Supplies

bandages (cloth or adhesive)
gauze
cotton swabs
tongue depressors (for splints)
empty sterilized pill bottles

Grooming Supplies

plastic tub (or empty water table)
empty plastic shampoo-type bottles
sponges
towels
hair dryer (cord removed)
brush
comb
toothbrush
ribbons
bandanas

Office Supplies

office sign (page 123)
patient forms (page 124)
appointment book
telephone
clipboard
dry pet treats

Tip!
Purchase a cardboard pet carrier for a minimal cost at a veterinary clinic or pet store. Explain how you plan to use the carrier, and it may be donated!

2. Introduce the theme

 Caring for Your Pets: A Book About Veterinarians written by Ann Owen and illustrated by Eric Thomas

Do You Have a Pet?
(sung to the tune of "Do Your Ears Hang Low?")

Do you have a cat?
Do you have a puppy dog?
Do you live with a hamster
Or take care of a frog?
Do you have a special friend who's a veterinarian?
Do you have a pet?

3. Suggest several roles

Receptionist	Answers telephone, greets pet owners and their pets, hands out patient forms, books appointments, confirms appointments
Pet Owner	Brings pet to office, fills out forms, describes symptoms
Veterinarian	Examines and treats pets
Vet Tech	Helps veterinarian
Groomer	Bathes and grooms pets

4. Inspire plenty of play

- Vary the selection of toy stuffed-animal patients.

- Every few days, suggest a different play scenario, such the following:
  — Offer a weeklong pet-grooming special that includes a bubble bath and a blow-dry (or brush).
  — All pets receive free dental checkups during Dental Health Day.
  — Arrange a pet show (all vaccinations must be up to date).
  — Get free and painless microchip implants (the rice-size implants that are helpful in returning lost pets to their owners).
  — Sign up for our pet owners' training class.

- Invite youngsters to share pet-related stories, photographs, pictures, and artwork during group time.

Happy Pets

Hooray for Dramatic Play! • ©The Mailbox® Books • TEC61312

Note to the teacher: Use with pages 121 and 122. Make a copy of page 124 for your files. Remove this mini poster and put it in a plastic page protector for durability. Then display it at the center at students' eye level.

Happy Pets

Pet's name _____

Reason for the visit:

Treatment (Check all that apply.)

⭕ bandage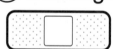

⭕ shot

⭕ medicine

⭕ bed rest

⭕ bath

⭕ other

Veterinarian _____

Hooray for Dramatic Play! • ©The Mailbox® Books • TEC61312

Note to the teacher: Use with pages 121 and 122. To save paper, laminate one or two copies of the page and provide an equal number of wipe-off markers.

Piggy Bank

Debit Card

232D O4IN 778R 934A

TEC61312

cardholder's name

Piggy Bank

Debit Card

532A 64IE 877X 593Z

TEC61312

cardholder's name

Piggy Bank

Debit Card

352F I6OG 7I7S 459I

TEC61312

cardholder's name

Piggy Bank

Debit Card

223B 46OT I78M 349H

TEC61312

cardholder's name

123

Date _____

Pay to _____ $ [ ]

Piggy Bank, USA _____

TEC61312

456

Date _____

Pay to _____ $ [ ]

Piggy Bank, USA _____

TEC61312

789

Date _____

Pay to _____ $ [ ]

Piggy Bank, USA _____

TEC61312

Customer name:

	Item	Price
I.		
2.		
3.		
	Total	

TEC61312

Customer name:

	Item	Price
I.		
2.		
3.		
	Total	

TEC61312